A TALE OF TWO CITIES

NOTES

including
- *Critical Biography of Dickens*
- *Introduction to the Novel*
- *List of Characters*
- *Brief Synopsis of the Novel*
- *Chapter Summaries*
- *Critical Commentaries of the Chapters*
- *Character Analyses*
- *Time Scheme of the Novel*
- *Genealogy*

by
James Weigel, Jr.

Cliffs Notes

INCORPORATED

LINCOLN, NEBRASKA 68501

Editor

Gary Carey, M.A.
University of Colorado

Consulting Editor

James L. Roberts, Ph.D.
Department of English
University of Nebraska

ISBN 0-8220-1255-3
© Copyright 1969, 1988
by
Cliffs Notes, Inc.
All Rights Reserved
Printed in U.S.A.

1996 Printing

Cliffs Notes, Inc.   Lincoln, Nebraska

CONTENTS

A Tale of Two Cities Notes

CRITICAL BIOGRAPHY OF DICKENS

There is something about Charles Dickens' imaginative power that defies explanation in purely biographical terms. Nevertheless, his biography shows the source of that power and is the best place to begin to define it.

The second child of John and Elizabeth Dickens, Charles was born on February 7, 1812, near Portsmouth on England's south coast. At that time John Dickens was stationed in Portsmouth as a clerk in the Navy Pay Office. The family was of lower-middle-class origins, John having come from servants and Elizabeth from minor bureaucrats. Dickens' father was vivacious and generous but had an unfortunate tendency to live beyond his means. His mother was affectionate and rather inept in practical matters. Dickens later used his father as the basis for Mr. Micawber and portrayed his mother as Mrs. Nickleby.

After a transfer to London in 1814, the family moved to Chatham, near Rochester, three years later. Dickens was about five at the time, and for the next five years his life was pleasant. Taught to read by his mother, he devoured his father's small collection of classics, which included Shakespeare, Cervantes, Defoe, Smollett, Fielding, and Goldsmith. These left a permanent mark on his imagination; their effect on his art was quite important. Dickens also went to some performances of Shakespeare and formed a lifelong attachment to the theater. He attended school during this period and showed himself to be a rather solitary, observant, good-natured child with some talent for comic routines, which his father encouraged. In retrospect Dickens looked upon these years as a kind of golden age. His first novel, *The Pickwick Papers*, is in part an attempt to recreate their idyllic nature: it rejoices in innocence and the youthful spirit, and its happiest scenes take place in that precise geographical area.

In the light of the family's move back to London, where financial difficulties overtook the Dickenses, the time in Chatham must have seemed glorious indeed. The family moved into the shabby suburb of Camden Town, and Dickens was taken out of school and set to menial jobs about the household. In time, to help augment the family income, Dickens was given a job in a blacking factory among rough companions. At the same time his father was imprisoned for debt, but was released three months later by a small legacy. Dickens related to his friend, John Forster, long afterward, that he felt a deep sense of abandonment at this time; the major themes of his novels can be traced to this period. His sympathy for the victimized, his fascination with prisons and money, the desire to vindicate his heroes' status as gentlemen, and the idea of London as an awesome, lively, and rather threatening environment all reflect these experiences. No doubt this temporary collapse of his parents' ability to protect him made a vivid impression on him. Out on his own for a time at twelve years of age, Dickens acquired a lasting self-reliance, a driving ambition, and a boundless energy that went into everything he did.

At thirteen Dickens went back to school for two years and then took a job in a lawyer's office. Dissatisfied with the work, he learned shorthand and became a freelance court reporter in 1828. The job was seasonal and allowed him to do a good deal of reading in the British Museum. At the age of twenty he became a full-fledged journalist, working for three papers in succession. In the next four or five years he acquired the reputation of being the fastest and most accurate parliamentary reporter in London. The value of this period was that Dickens gained a sound, firsthand knowledge of London and the provinces.

In December, 1833, Dickens began to publish sketches of London and its inhabitants in the *Monthly Magazine*. Later he signed them with the pseudonym, "Boz," and became known for the dramatic quality of his reportage, achieving a modest degree of fame. On his twenty-fourth birthday the articles were published in book form as *Sketches by Boz, Illustrative of Everyday Life and Everyday People*. Although the book was a success, it had minimal intrinsic literary merit, at least in comparison to the novels that were to follow. Nonetheless, it launched him on his career as a writer, a career astonishing in its productivity, quality, and undiminished popular acclaim.

It is a mistake to think of Dickens as an uneducated man merely because he had little formal schooling. The truth is that Dickens never stopped learning. His entire writing career was a continuous process of development and experimentation. It is true that certain themes keep reappearing in his works and that these themes almost certainly stem from his early life. But Dickens worked them over in novel after novel until they took on the symbolic complexity, the depth, and the social perceptiveness of great art. Borrowing the melodramatic conventions of his day, Dickens transmuted them into towering and popular novels that were capable of portraying a whole society. From *The Pickwick Papers* to *The Mystery of Edwin Drood* Dickens never ceased to develop, establishing himself as the major Victorian novelist.

A week after his first book was published, the firm of Chapman and Hall approached Dickens about writing a series of sporting sketches to accompany illustrations by a well-known artist. Dickens convinced the firm that the drawings should arise from the text, and he began writing the first installment of *The Posthumous Papers of the Pickwick Club*, which appeared in April, 1836. Writing in monthly installments was a mode of publication that proved congenial to Dickens. In the beginning it enabled him to continue his newspaper work and later to edit magazines. But if this manner of writing for deadlines inflicted a certain lack of artistic unity on his early novels, he was able in time to overcome his episodic structures and impose a tighter, more coherent organization on his novels.

The Pickwick Papers did not sell well at first, but with the introduction of Sam Weller sales skyrocketed into the tens of thousands. A Pickwick rage started, which assured Dickens' success. On the surface this novel is a series of sketches that are loosely held together by the adventures of Samuel Pickwick and his friends. Yet there are certain basic themes that unify the novel: the celebration of travel, benevolence, youthfulness, friendship, and plenty; the contrast between the freedom of the open road and the constriction of Fleet Prison; the comic view of marriage; and the gradual revelation of Mr. Pickwick's endearing humanity.

With the prospect of a livable income Dickens, at twenty-four, married Catherine Hogarth, the daughter of a newspaper colleague. The marriage was probably happy enough in its first years, and certainly prolific: there were ten children. Catherine seems to have been a placid, gentle, affectionate woman, but she was rather commonplace and without much aptitude for housekeeping. Under the strain of personality conflicts, the pressure of Dickens' numerous activities, and his infatuation with Ellen Ternan, the couple separated twenty-two years later.

While still working on *The Pickwick Papers* (1836-37) Dickens contracted to write two more novels and began publishing *Oliver Twist* (1837-38). During this time he also worked on a second series of *Sketches by Boz* (1839). *Oliver Twist* was a new departure for Dickens, presenting an attack on workhouse and slum conditions and a picture of London criminals through the nightmarish experiences of an innocent young boy. Oliver's trials are rewarded in the end when his claim to gentility is established beyond question. Before he had completed that novel Dickens had begun *Nicholas Nickleby* (1838-39), an exposé of schools for unwanted boys. The hero this time actively seeks a gentlemanly position in life, whereas Oliver was largely passive. The workhouse, the crime-infested slum, the private school are all degrading environments, and the only proper alternative is gentility. Dickens was intensely concerned with status, and in these two novels the main conflict is between those who try to deprive the hero of it and those who abet him. Undoubtedly, Dickens had hit upon a new theme that interested a considerable proportion of the English middle class.

Dickens' next novel, *The Old Curiosity Shop* (1840-41), increased his popularity and stunned the public with the sentimentalized death of Little Nell. The heroine's impulse to leave London in order to find a pastoral security and peace may be an urge toward death. The city, for all its sinister aspects, was to Dickens a center of vitality, while the countryside was rich in graveyards and moldering churches.

Dickens, even at this early stage in his career, was capable of ambiguous feelings about the central subjects of his novels. He wrote about things that made him uneasy, that raised questions in his mind. His novels were attempts to answer those questions about the city, prison, money, crime, success, gentility, and death. Time and again he came back to these subjects because his questions were of a kind that can never be answered conclusively.

Barnaby Rudge (1841) revolved about the anti-Catholic riots of 1780 and probed the relationship between vicious or misguided parental authority and the obtuse, often selfish, authority of public institutions. Here Dickens begins to move from the personal level to the societal level, finding correspondences between the two. This was a method he would develop to perfection in his later novels. In this, his first historical novel, Dickens matched Sir Walter Scott at his own genre.

In 1842 Dickens and his wife made a trip to America, which resulted in *American Notes* (1842), an unflattering travel book, and in the novel, *Martin Chuzzlewit* (1843-44). If this picaresque tale is structurally flawed, it explores various types of egoism and hypocrisy with extraordinary verve. Again, the action centers on the hero's efforts to establish himself in the world. But he is the first hero of Dickens to have a serious character flaw, that of selfishness.

With *Dombey and Son* (1846-48) Dickens took pride as his theme—the pride of power and position that marked certain commercial magnates—and used this to show the forces of social change in the Victorian world. Mr. Dombey's inhuman pride is gradually humbled by the death of his only son, his wife's elopement with his manager, and the collapse of his commercial empire. Simultaneously, one can see the growing power of industry as opposed to the waning power of mercantile interests. Technically, this novel is much superior to Dickens' earlier works and marks the beginning of his mature art, but at the same time his comic inventiveness is subdued. As Dickens' organizational skill grew in his successive novels, his comic flair diminished into satire.

For his eighth novel, *David Copperfield* (1849-50), he made use of autobiographical material. Copperfield's early hardship and later rise to prominence is a thinly disguised version of Dickens' own life. This was Dickens' first attempt to show a hero's education from the inside, with a first-person narrative. The interest of the book, as a result, lies in the peripheral characters and intrigues, which form the raw material of Copperfield's growth.

What one notices is that each novel builds on the previous ones and yet is an effort at something new and fresh. In *Bleak House* (1852-53), for example, he used chancery and its legal obfuscations to serve as a metaphor for the confusions of society at large, and to connect every level of society from the aristocratic Dedlocks to Jo the street-sweeper. Moreover, he set an omniscient third-person narrative side by side with a personal narrator to get a dual vision of the Victorian mental climate, a vision both inclusive and intimate. This experimentation served to enhance his popularity, yet it was a very important element in his artistic greatness as well.

In *Hard Times* (1854) Dickens combined the moral fable with realistic social analysis in the depiction of an industrial town. The factory and the school are the confining and objective equivalents of the narrow statistical views of the English political economists. As an alternative to the social prison Dickens presents the freedom and goodwill of a circus troupe. As Dickens grew older one notices in his books that benevolence has a harder time of it. It is no longer handed out freely by pleasant gentlemen of unlimited means. It becomes increasingly personal, the expression of love in an ever more hostile world.

Dickens' following novel, *Little Dorrit* (1855-57), allows no alternative to the vision of society as a series of interrelated prisons. From top to bottom all the world's a jail, and no one can escape its influence. The best that can be salvaged from this cramped, claustrophobic society is the tender affection between Arthur Clennam and Amy Dorrit, both of whom are overshadowed by the Marshalsea Prison.

However, in *A Tale of Two Cities* (1859) we see society crumbling into anarchy because of its prison-like nature. A political and religious parable, this novel places society's regeneration in friendship, in the family, and in heroic self-sacrifice, each of which is based on love.

Prison also plays a part in *Great Expectations* (1860-61). Most of the characters, including Pip, the hero-narrator, are corrupted by money and the things it can purchase. Crime and prison are simply the most dramatic forms of that corruption. Here Dickens returned to his early theme of the young man trying to make good as a gentleman, but this time the treatment is shot through with irony and social insight. Pip's snobbish rise in the world is based on a convict's money. In this novel Dickens shows that redemption lies in good, honest work.

Our Mutual Friend (1864-65) was Dickens' last completed novel. It, too, deals with the corrupting taint of money, but on a panoramic scale with a third-person narrative. The whole Victorian world is indicted, and once more Dickens stresses the regenerating force of love. This was his final attempt to portray society on a grand scale.

The last novel, *The Mystery of Edwin Drood* (1870), remained unfinished. It turns away from society, if not from prison, and concentrates on private pathology, on the double nature of a murderer. It is almost Dostoevskian in its depiction of the criminal as a man tormented and fallen from grace, and yet a man who can assume a mask of respectability. This was characteristic of Dickens; that the novel on which he was working at the time of his death should be still another new departure. *Edwin Drood* is a tantalizing piece of work.

Dickens' body of novels is his outstanding achievement, an enduring testament to his enormous, intense creative life. But he wrote much else besides: volumes of good journalistic articles, two travel books, thousands of letters, a book of Christmas stories, a history of England for children. In addition, he edited three magazines, two of these for many years.

Dickens was also involved in the theater all of his adult life. He attended plays frequently and, for a time, considered becoming a professional actor. He wrote plays, acted in amateur productions (which were quite skilled), and directed them with an impressive energy and thoroughness. In time his theatrical bent found an outlet in public readings from his novels. These readings were extremely successful, and Dickens overwhelmed his audiences. But the strain of all this hastened his death.

Dickens practiced benevolence as well as wrote about it, doing many favors for his family and numerous relatives. He organized public charities with the heiress, Angela Burdett-Coutts, and helped at benefits, contributing substantial sums.

Dickens was very active physically. He loved taking long walks, riding horses, making journeys, entertaining friends, dining well, playing practical jokes. He enjoyed games of charades with his family, was an excellent amateur magician, and practiced hypnotism. One tends to share Shaw's opinion that Dickens, in his social life, was always on stage. He was like an eternal Master of Ceremonies, for the most part: flamboyant, observant, quick, dynamic, full of zest. Yet he was also restless, subject to fits of depression, and hot tempered, so that at times he must have been nearly intolerable to live with, however agreeable he was as a companion.

Dickens' domestic life, in fact, was somewhat irregular. The man who sentimentalized and exalted conjugal happiness was quite prone to falling in love with other women, including his sisters-in-law, Mary and Georgina Hogarth. His relationship with Miss Ternan, while probably platonic at first, became overtly erotic, and she became his mistress after he separated from his wife. Nor was Dickens the indulgent father that his novels might lead us to expect. Whereas in fiction he caused his readers to weep over the fates of innocent and victimized children, he was in actuality rather harsh to his own children. Dickens, after all, like many men accustomed to vigorous activity and the public limelight, was very impatient and spoiled. He wanted much attention, and between his own demands and those of his ten children his marriage naturally fell to pieces. However, this does not mean that Dickens was an out-and-out hypocrite. What he projected in his novels was what most men dream of having at home: a comforting, tidy, affectionate, attentive wife. And he understood a child's sense of lostness in an incomprehensible world, which he dramatized in fiction. Everyone knows this same feeling, but very few are quick to recognize it in others. Dickens was no exception in this insensitivity.

In view of his very strenuous life it was not surprising that he died at fifty-eight from a stroke. At his death on June 9, 1870, Dickens was wealthy, immensely popular, and the best novelist the Victorian age produced. He was buried in the Poet's Corner of Westminster Abbey, and people mourned his death the world over.

INTRODUCTION TO *A TALE OF TWO CITIES*

Published serially in *All the Year Round* from April 30 to November 29, 1859, *A Tale of Two Cities* has long been one of Dickens' most favored books, rivaling *David Copperfield, Oliver Twist,* and *The Pickwick Papers* in the public esteem. Besides offering a swift, exciting story and a memorable rendering of the French Revolution, the novel has two unforgettable characters: Sydney Carton and Madame Defarge. Each has become fixed in the common imagination, and each is as vivid as the actual historical figures of the French Revolution; this is because they have the dramatic intensity that fiction gives. However, it is essentially a serious novel.

Its position in the canon of Dickens' fourteen completed novels is somewhere near the bottom in most critical estimates, right around *Nicholas Nickleby* and *Barnaby Rudge*. But few critics have paid much attention to it, and when they have their approaches have been curiously unfruitful. The novel rightfully belongs somewhere among the works of middle quality. If it lacks the richness of character and invention of Dickens' masterpieces, it still possesses their structural and thematic unity. It is much better organized than Dickens' first six novels, but it pays for this in the starkness of its mood and form. In this respect, it shares the darkening tone of Dickens' late works.

Of all Dickens' novels *A Tale of Two Cities* is closest in subject matter to *Barnaby Rudge*, his first historical novel. In both novels Dickens explores, among other things, the relation of private grievance to public violence. The mob in *Barnaby Rudge* that storms and burns Newgate Prison is the prototype of the mob that attacks the Bastille in *A Tale of Two Cities*, except that in the former novel the riots are put down eventually. The injustices behind the French Revolution are shown to be much more serious than those behind the Gordon riots of 1780. By the time Dickens wrote *A Tale of Two Cities* his craftsmanship had matured enough to enable him to grapple with one of the most important historical events of all time.

Dickens' literary influences in this book range from folklore, which contributes a mythical dimension to the characters and a tautness to the structure; to the New Testament, which provides the morality of the story; to eighteenth- and nineteenth-century melodrama, which influenced Dickens' manner of drawing his scenes; to Carlyle, whose study of the French Revolution provided Dickens with a rationale for treating the same subject. Dickens was also closely indebted to Bulwer-Lytton's novel, *Zanoni*, and to Watt Phillip's play, *The Dead Heart*, for certain aspects of his plot and characters. Both works used the French Revolution as a background. Nevertheless, Dickens was no mere imitator. He used these sources naturally, as part of his own imaginative makeup; and *A Tale of Two Cities* carries an authenticity of vision, a personal directness and force, that is entirely Dickens'.

To deduce Dickens' personality from his novels is particularly hazardous, yet this novel reflects some of the stresses of his life. It has been said that Dickens identified with Charles Darnay, who bears his initials and first name, and with Sydney Carton, who is supposed to be a dramatization of Dickens' love for Ellen Ternan in 1859. But if this is so, Dickens was eating his cake and having it too, since Darnay marries Lucie while Carton worships her and Dickens had his Ellen.

A more solid case can be made of Dickens' sympathy for Dr. Manette. Manette's duality parallels Dickens'. His persevering, vigorous work as a physician has its counterpart in Dickens' work as a journalistic reformer, which was quite literally a means of promoting society's health. And Dr. Manette's insane cobbling, which he learned while unjustly imprisoned, is part of an attempt by Manette to create an imaginary world for himself when reality becomes too threatening, similar in a sense to Dickens' creation of an imaginary world in his novels. Both sides of Dickens' personality are represented here in a disguised form, the outward reformer and the interior fiction-maker.

Dickens' explicit social ideas in this novel are rudimentary. They amount to no more than this: the French Revolution was inevitable because the aristocracy exploited and plundered the poor until they were driven to revolt. Thus, oppression on a large scale results in anarchy. And anarchy in turn produces a police state. One of Dickens' strongest convictions was that the English people might erupt at any moment into a mass of bloody revolutionists. It is clear now that he was mistaken, but the idea was firmly planted in his mind, as well as in the minds of his contemporaries. A *Tale of Two Cities* was partly an attempt to show his readers the dangers of a possible revolution. This was not the first time a simple — and incorrect — conviction became the occasion for a serious and powerful work of art.

This does not mean that Dickens' fears of revolution in England were unfounded. In the 1830s and 1840s the dissatisfactions of industrial workers reached alarming national proportions with the Chartist movement; and the unemployed were always a threat. But Chartism had lost much of its force by the 1850s owing to an increase in general prosperity. However, Dickens felt the roots of rebellion remained untouched. Almost all of Europe was caught up in violent revolutionary activity during the first half of the nineteenth century, and it was natural for middle-class Englishmen to fear that widespread rebellion might take place at home. Dickens knew what poverty was like and how common it was. He realized how inadequate philanthropic institutions were, confronted by the enormous misery of the slums. It is not surprising that Dickens turned to the French Revolution to dramatize the possibility of class uprisings. Few events in history offered such a concentration of terrors.

If the terrors of the Revolution take a political form, the hope that Dickens holds out in this novel has distinct religious qualities. In a very basic way *A Tale of Two Cities* is a fable about resurrection. And the central figure of the fable is Sydney Carton, who re-enacts figuratively the expiatory death of Christ. However, Dickens puts the Christian doctrine of salvation on a secular basis, leading not to an other-worldly Heaven but to the survival of Carton's friends and to the regeneration of society. These matters will be taken up more fully later on. At this point it is sufficient to note that in this book Dickens drew on a hope that is perennial, that is in fact necessary to the life of the spirit. Resurrection is one of the great abiding themes of Western literature.

LIST OF CHARACTERS

Jarvis Lorry

An agent of Tellson's Bank. Elderly, neatly but quaintly dressed, he befriends the Manettes, for whom he performs many valuable services.

Lucie Manette, later Darnay

A pretty, blonde young woman who has a compassionate nature and the power to inspire great love and loyalty in others.

Dr. Alexandre Manette

Lucie's father, a prisoner for nearly eighteen years in the Bastille. He gradually recovers from his imprisonment with the aid of his daughter and later tries to pay her back by rescuing her husband, Charles Darnay, from the guillotine.

Miss Pross

A big, redheaded, mannish Englishwoman who serves as Lucie Manette's nurse and protector.

Ernest Defarge

A big, stolid owner of a wineshop in Paris. Later he becomes an official and leader in the French Revolution.

Madame Thérèse Defarge

The wife of Ernest Defarge, a fierce, vindictive, impassive woman who waits for the Revolution so that she can inflict vengeance on her enemies and the upper classes. She knits the names of her intended victims and exemplifies the driving force behind the Revolution.

Jacques One, Two, Three, and Four

A secret society of revolutionaries who plan and precipitate the French Revolution.

Jeremy (Jerry) Cruncher

The porter at Tellson's and Jarvis Lorry's errand-man, a rough, surly, comic figure who is secretly a body-snatcher.

Mrs. Cruncher

Jerry's wife, a pious woman who is frequently beaten by her husband for praying.

Young Jerry Cruncher

The son, a small, nasty version of the father. He assists his father at Tellson's and aspires to be a body-snatcher.

Charles Darnay

A French exile in England, he earns a living as a tutor and courts and marries Lucie Manette. He is put on trial a number of times. Motivated by family honor and the desire to expiate his family's crimes, he keeps being imprisoned, from which he must be rescued.

Sydney Carton

A drunken, dissipated lawyer who looks like Charles Darnay and who rescues his double from execution twice because of his own devotion to Lucie.

C. J. Stryver

Darnay's defense lawyer in England and Sydney Carton's employer; he is a gross, portly, ambitious boor.

Roger Cly

A police spy in England who informs against Darnay and later a prison spy in Revolutionary France.

John Barsad, or Solomon Pross

A police spy in England who also informs against Darnay and who becomes a prison spy in Revolutionary France. He helps Carton save Darnay.

Monseigneur the Marquis

A greedy, mercenary French aristocrat whose goods and property are confiscated during the Revolution.

Marquis St. Evrémonde

Darnay's wicked uncle, a predatory aristocrat who is murdered by a revolutionist.

Gabelle

The steward of the Evrémondes and a local tax collector who is imprisoned and released during the Revolution.

Gaspard

The assassin of the Marquis St. Evrémonde after the Marquis ran his child down.

Road-mender and Wood-sawyer

A man initiated into the revolutionary movement by the Defarges and who becomes a bloodthirsty revolutionist.

Young Lucie Darnay

The child of Lucie and Charles Darnay who is taken to France during the Reign of Terror because her father is imprisoned there.

Foulon

An arrogant aristocrat who is hanged after the storming of the Bastille.

The Vengeance

A murderous revolutionist who becomes Madame Defarge's female henchman.

A Seamstress

A pathetic young woman who was sentenced to be executed with Darnay and who sees through Carton's imposture. She and Carton comfort each other on the way to the guillotine.

BRIEF SYNOPSIS

In 1775 Jarvis Lorry is sent by his firm, Tellson's Bank, on a confidential mission to Paris. His object is to find Dr. Alexandre Manette, a physician who had spent eighteen years in the Bastille, and return with him to England. Mr. Lorry is accompanied by Dr. Manette's daughter, Lucie, who learns for the first time that her father is alive. At Paris they go to Defarge's wineshop and discover the doctor in a dreadful state. Deranged after his long prison term, he is withdrawn, lacking memory, and prematurely aged. His only activity is cobbling shoes. Dr. Manette is induced to journey to London with his daughter and Mr. Lorry. There they hope to restore him to sanity and health.

Five years later, in 1780, the three of them are called as witnesses in a trial at Old Bailey. The defendant, Charles Darnay, is a Frenchman living in England and earning a livelihood by tutoring. However, his trips between the two countries have led to an accusation of treason. Lucie Manette reluctantly gives damaging circumstantial evidence against him. But the prosecution's case falters when a witness cannot positively identify Darnay because of his likeness to Sydney Carton, a lawyer in the courtroom. So Darnay is acquitted.

Both Carton and Darnay are enamored of Lucie and call on her at home. Carton, who leads a drunken and uncertain life, regards his courtship as hopeless; but he professes his love to Lucie and his willingness to sacrifice himself for her. Darnay of course wins out, and he and Lucie are married with her father's uneasy blessing. Dr. Manette, who has regained enough vigor and sanity to set up a medical practice, suffers a nine-day relapse after the wedding.

In France the aristocracy has gradually sapped the country's resources, reducing the people to dreadful poverty. The people, under increasing oppression, start preparing for vengeance and revolution. Shortly after his carriage kills a child, the Marquis St. Evrémonde, Darnay's suave, callous uncle, is assassinated at his château. Darnay inherits the estate but he renounces it, preferring to live modestly in England than to exploit the French peasantry as his uncle had done. In 1789 the people revolt, storming the Bastille, burning châteaux, and murdering or imprisoning the members of the former régime.

In 1792, with the French Revolution in full fury, Darnay receives a plea for help from his family steward, Gabelle, who has been jailed. After eleven years of happy married life, and the birth of a daughter, Darnay feels he has neglected responsibilities in France, and he decides to return to his native country. Without telling his wife he leaves for France, where he is immediately seized and jailed as an enemy of the state.

Lucie and her daughter and Dr. Manette arrive in Paris soon after, hoping to assist Darnay if they can. Mr. Lorry is also present, taking care of Tellson's French office. Darnay's trial is delayed for over a year. When Darnay's trial finally comes up Dr. Manette's plea secures an acquittal, for as one of the former prisoners in the Bastille, Manette has been made a folk hero of the Revolution.

Darnay is unexpectedly re-arrested that same day because of Madame Defarge, a leading revolutionist who wants to exterminate the entire Evrémonde family for personal reasons. On the following day Charles Darnay is tried, convicted, and sentenced to death by the Tribunal. His father-in-law, Dr. Manette, knows the situation is hopeless; and, shattered by the trial, reverts to his old demented state.

Sydney Carton, arriving in Paris, learns of Darnay's new trial and impending execution. He also overhears a plot against the lives of Lucie and her daughter and father. Acting quickly, Carton tells Mr. Lorry to have a carriage prepared an hour before the execution. Then, having access to the prison through a spy and informer, Carton enters Darnay's cell, drugs him, and changes places with him. The deception works because of the striking resemblance between the two men. Under Mr. Lorry's protection Darnay, his wife and child and father-in-law, successfully escape from France while Carton goes to the guillotine, a sacrifice prompted by his intense, pure love for Lucie Darnay.

Just before he is beheaded Sydney Carton has a prophetic vision of a better society emerging from the holocaust and of his own survival in the memories of the Darnay family, and he faces death in serenity and triumph.

SUMMARIES AND COMMENTARIES

BOOK I

Summary

In 1775 people viewed their era as exceptionally good or exceptionally wicked, as millennial or apocalyptic. Both England and France had undistinguished kings, and in each country the status quo was generally accepted as an eternal truth.

France was marked by a harsh and repressive social system in which inflation was rampant and in which a man could be tortured and put to death for not bowing to a procession of monks. Even then changes were taking place that would turn timber into guillotines and farm carts into tumbrils.

England had its faults as well. Burglary and holdups were everyday occurrences, and violence was very common. The English were about to experience a revolution, too, in America. Yet complacency was the order of the day everywhere, the result of a blindness to actual social conditions.

The Dover mail coach is slogging its way at night through mud and fog in November, 1775. The passengers and coachmen are very suspicious and fearful because of the probability of highwaymen. A messenger from Tellson's Bank in London rides up and asks for Jarvis Lorry, an agent of the Bank. After being identified as "Jerry" by Mr. Lorry, the messenger tells Mr. Lorry that he is to wait for a young woman in Dover. Mr. Lorry, in return, gives Jerry a message for the Bank, "Recalled to life," which puzzles the messenger and makes him uneasy as he rides back to London. Meanwhile Mr. Lorry dozes in his coach and dreams of literally exhuming a man and questioning him on his will to live after having been buried for nearly eighteen years.

Mr. Lorry stops at a hotel in Dover where he refreshes himself and waits for the young lady, Miss Lucie Manette, whom he is to take to Paris. Mr. Lorry, who is sixty and a bachelor, thinks of himself purely as a businessman, but in his interview with Miss Manette it is evident that he is full of tact and goodwill. He explains to Lucie that her father, whom she has never seen and whom she believes to be dead, is alive in Paris after a long imprisonment and that they are going to rescue him in circumstances of secrecy: Mr. Lorry as an agent of Tellson's and Lucie to nurse him back to health. She is anxious about meeting her father and faints, whereupon Lucie's nurse rushes into the room, flings Mr. Lorry against the wall, and coddles Miss Manette back to consciousness.

Paris is oppressed with hunger and poverty, and the breaking of a wine cask in the street inspires a brief celebration in which the people of the neighborhood scoop and sop up the wine to drink it. However, one man uses the muddied wine to write "BLOOD" on a wall—a joke which the wineshop owner, Ernest Defarge, sternly reproves.

Going back into his shop Defarge finds Mr. Lorry and Lucie waiting for him to guide them to her father, Alexandre Manette. His wife, Madame Defarge, stonily sits at her knitting, directing the affairs of the shop by slight gestures, apparently noticing nothing. After three men who call one another "Jacques" leave the shop Mr. Lorry informs Defarge of his mission. The thought of Dr. Manette's unjust imprisonment angers Defarge as he leads the pair up to the garret. Outside the room they find the three "Jacques" peeping at Dr. Manette through chinks, and Defarge explains that he shows the man only to select people. As they enter the room Mr. Lorry has to support Lucie Manette, since she is about to faint. In the gloom they view an old man busy cobbling shoes.

Dr. Manette is clearly mad. Haggard and prematurely aged (he is forty-five years old), eighteen years in prison have reduced him to a cipher whose sole identity is his cell number. He cannot recall his past or even his name. Yet the sight of his daughter stimulates a fleeting memory of his wife, and he instinctively turns to her for comfort. Lucie urges him to weep for his lost wife and home, for his long imprisonment and wasted possibilities. He does so but the effort exhausts him and he sinks to the floor. Lucie tends him while Defarge and Mr. Lorry make

preparations for his journey to England on the following day.
Finally Mr. Lorry, Lucie and her father leave for London; and
Mr. Lorry wonders about Dr. Manette's chances for recovery.

Commentary

In his memorable opening sentences Dickens creates an
effective rhetoric out of sheer platitudes, which dramatize the
atmosphere of complacency that he wants to project. They also
prepare one for the brisk, clipped, almost breathless prose style
that characterizes this novel.

By describing the kings of England and France (both unnamed) simply as men with large jaws Dickens employs a favorite
device of his: seizing upon a physical trait to suggest mental qualities; in this case, each king's mediocrity, his empty talk, and his
virtual interchangeability with the other. In doing so Dickens
ridicules the outmoded notion of the divine right of kings, which
received its death-blow in the French Revolution.

Dickens has no sentimental attachment to the "good old
days." In comparing France's authoritarian society with the law-
lessness in England he makes the two countries mirror-images of
each other, balancing the semi-totalitarian against the semi-
anarchic, and England comes off little better than France. However, politics are of secondary interest here. Dickens is more
concerned with the contingencies of daily life in his portrayal
of the period.

Dickens intends the isolation of the passengers, coachmen,
and bank messenger to serve as a metaphor for everyone. In the
opening passage of Chapter 3 Dickens asserts that all people are
mysterious secrets to one another, and that this intimate secrecy
is connected in some way with the enigma of death. What
Dickens is getting at here is not the modern concept of aliena-
tion but rather the normal human mystery of being locked in
one's own skin and mind, of being vulnerable and mortal. The
coach passengers are bundled up physically and mentally, and
are suspicious, secretive, and ready for violence. In this emotional climate Mr. Lorry has the morbid dream about digging up a
dead man.

Chapters 2 and 3 set forth a puzzle to create suspense: how
can a dead man (or one who has been buried alive for many

years) be revivified? Part of the answer is provided in Chapter 4: he has not been buried in actuality, he has been imprisoned. But a prison for Dickens, who visited many of them in his lifetime, was a kind of living death if one's term was prolonged. Thus, in Chapter 3 Dickens moves from normal human isolation to the intense solitude that prison inflicts on a man, which is represented in Mr. Lorry's dreaming as being a form of burial.

The title and motif of the first book of this novel, "Recalled to Life," is also the major theme. A *Tale of Two Cities* is fundamentally concerned with resurrection—the release of people from the Kingdom of Death and from their own isolation. The puzzle of the burial, as stated above, is therefore the initial announcement of what the novel is about.

In reading Dickens one should pay particular attention to small details, since these often reveal the basic concerns of the novelist. For example, in the room in which the interview between Lucie Manette and Mr. Lorry takes place (which itself is dark and funereal) the light reflected from the candles on the oiled mahogany table seems "buried." And the black cupids that adorn the frame of a mirror in the room are either headless or maimed, which is the first image of decapitation and which prefigures the final vision of the guillotine.

The specific prison of course is the Bastille, which so far remains unnamed, as if its reality were so overwhelming that to name it would subtract some of its dread power. The action of Book I is the rescue of Dr. Manette from the proximity of the prison, and is the first of several rescues.

The revelation of Dr. Manette's dementia is the climax to which the preceding events move smoothly and swiftly. Yet the effect of this climax falters when Lucie Manette's reaction to her father turns into the worst kind of sentimental melodrama as she repeats the bathetic formula, "Weep for it, weep for it!" Dickens and his readers loved these tearful scenes between parent and child. Their stylized nature shows an indebtedness to the Victorian stage. Throughout the novel we see Dickens managing his characters like a theater director, emphasizing the dramatic gesture, the physical trait, the coincidence, as though his tremendous energy must inevitably explode in action, whether comic or melodramatic. Even in his grotesque moments, such as Mr. Lorry's questioning of the dead man in his dream, Dickens converts the morbid into something spirited and purposeful.

Book I possesses the structural and tonal unity of a long short story. There is a single plot that moves quickly to its climax and an emotional mood that is sustained and intensified (with a lapse or two) right to the end. However, one is always aware that this section is just the prologue to the novel. The theme of resurrection is announced; and geographically, the movement from England to France and back again prefigures the action of the rest of the novel. Moreover, Dickens takes pains to insert curious, unresolved elements that foreshadow future events. The word "BLOOD" and Defarge's secret society of "Jacquerie" point to the French Revolution. And this section ends on a question: can good care and the affection of his daughter bring Dr. Manette back to bodily and mental health?

BOOK II

Summary

Tellson's Bank is a cramped, dark, ugly, and inconvenient establishment next to Temple Bar. It is run by shriveled old men who take pride in its detriments, in its resistance to change, and in its musty aura of senescence and decay. When it took young men into its employ it seemed to hide them until they were old. It upholds the harsh criminal law of the time by which three-fourths of all offenses were punishable by death, and in the course of time Tellson's has been responsible for many such deaths.

The odd-job man and porter at Tellson's is Jerry Cruncher (the mounted messenger of Book I, Chapter 2). He wakes one morning to find his wife praying and throws his boot at her on the assumption that her prayers are no better than curses designed to wreck his livelihood. His son, "Young Jerry," assists him with his work at Tellson's. A smaller version of his father, he is just as coarse and brutal. After forbidding his wife to pray Jerry leaves for his post in a surly mood, and his son goes with him.

Jerry Cruncher is sent by Tellson's to wait on Mr. Lorry at Old Bailey, where a trial for treason is taking place. The penalty for treason is quartering, a punishment that Cruncher finds barbarous; but he takes the same morbid interest in the proceedings as the crowd of spectators in the courtroom and jostles others to get a good view.

The prisoner, Charles Darnay, is a self-possessed young Frenchman whose journeys between England and France in a time of enmity have brought him under suspicion. Also in the courtroom and of interest to the crowd are Lucie Manette and her father, who are to appear, along with Mr. Lorry, as witnesses for the prosecution.

The prosecution's case is largely circumstantial, relying heavily on the testimony of two scoundrels acting as police spies. To buttress their accusations the prosecution calls on Lucie Manette to give an account of a conversation that took place between her and Darnay on the trip to England five years earlier. Lucie is very distressed and faint at having to testify against Darnay, but she takes pains not to conceal her incriminating evidence. The final witness, an unidentified man, swears to having seen Darnay near an army post before a trip to France, supposedly gathering information. His identification is shattered when the defense counsel points out Darnay's resemblance to Sydney Carton, a carelessly dressed, dissipated barrister present in the courtroom. The judge sums up the evidence in a manner that is prejudiced against Darnay, and the jury retires to deliberate. Lucie swoons and is taken out of the courtroom. Darnay, who has fallen in love with her, sends her a considerate message while his life hangs by a thread. The jury finally returns with an acquittal, and the disappointed crowd leaves.

The trial over, Darnay meets Lucie, Dr. Manette, Mr. Lorry, and the defense lawyer (a portly, aggressive man named C. J. Stryver) in a corridor of Old Bailey. They congratulate him on his release, but Dr. Manette gives Darnay a look of dislike and fear. Much improved in five years, though still subject to moments of abstraction, Dr. Manette is tired after the trial, so he and Lucie leave for home. Sydney Carton comes forward then and, after angering Mr. Lorry by his careless attitude, suggests that he and Darnay go to a restaurant nearby. Darnay feels ill at ease with his coarsened, alcoholic double but agrees to go. Carton drinks himself into a stupor, revealing in the meantime an antipathy to Darnay, whom he regards as a fortunate and enviable version of himself. Carton also likes Lucie Manette and feels a hopeless rivalry with Darnay. Darnay pays the bill and leaves Carton, who falls asleep with the candle dripping over him.

Sydney Carton has an unofficial partnership with Mr. Stryver, Darnay's defense lawyer, who has a pushy knack for getting on in the world but who needs Carton's intellectual gift for getting to the heart of a case. Both drink a good deal, Carton from frustration and Stryver because he enjoys it. During a brief-reading session it turns out that Carton really engineered Darnay's defense while Stryver took the credit for the victory. Stryver proposes a toast to Lucie and mentions her beauty, but Carton remarks that she is not pretty but rather a golden doll. However, Carton goes to bed drunk and tearful, knowing how inept he is at pursuing his own interests.

Mr. Lorry, now a close family friend of the Manettes, is a Sunday visitor at their apartment in Soho. About four months after the trial he finds Miss Pross alone in the house, and he inquires about Dr. Manette's state of mind from Lucie's old nurse, the same woman who had flung him against the wall in Dover five years before. He learns that the doctor, who has established a medical practice, is sometimes agitated and withdrawn. Secretly afraid of losing his identity again, Dr. Manette represses all memories of prison. Miss Pross, a short-tempered but good-hearted woman, is devoted to Lucie and jealous of her suitors. Dr. Manette and Lucie return and the four go out into the courtyard, but when Charles Darnay turns up, Miss Pross retires in a huff.

Darnay happens to mention an anecdote about a prisoner in the Tower of London who buried some papers in his cell. This story disturbs Dr. Manette, but it starts to rain and the group goes into the house.

Sydney Carton drops in for tea during the storm. He appears moody and is inclined to keep to himself. Lucie speaks of a premonition she has that the disembodied footsteps passing the house signify people who will someday enter their lives. And Carton gives this fancy an ominous turn by remarking that he sees a great crowd bearing down on the whole group.

In his Parisian suite Monseigneur, an influential member of the ruling oligarchy, takes his morning chocolate from four serving-men while various members of high society congregate in his reception rooms. These people are notable for their ennui and uselessness. Each is engaged in some occupation in which he has no belief, and of which he knows nothing. Pretense governs all conversation, and everyone is dressed as if for a fancy ball. Monseigneur, who sits in his private chamber, is famous for his private and public selfishness and for his indifference to the welfare of France. He makes a brief appearance among the courtiers, commending some and ignoring others, and then retires into his private chamber while his sycophants disperse.

One petitioner, the Marquis St. Evrémonde, is treated coldly and privately wishes Monseigneur to the devil. While riding furiously in his carriage through an impoverished suburb of Paris, Evrémonde accidentally kills a child. Unconcerned either with the death or the father's grief, the Marquis coldly tosses two gold coins at the father and Defarge, who is also in the crowd. His composure is shaken, however, when one of the coins is thrown back in defiance. Wishing he could trample the entire crowd, he drives off. The fancy ball of high society follows the Marquis and rides past that exact spot in fashionable carriages.

En route from Paris to the Evrémonde country estate both the crops and the people are poor and withered. The carriage stops in a village not far from the estate, and the Marquis questions a road-mender who claims he saw a man riding under the carriage. Driving on, the Marquis passes a graveyard where a grief-stricken woman begs him for a marker for the grave of her dead husband. But she is shoved away, and the carriage arrives at the estate in darkness.

The Marquis enters his château, a place of stone that is decorated with stone human and lion heads, and urns and balustrades. He inquires if his nephew has arrived, and on learning that he has not the Marquis prepares for dinner in his room, where he senses something at the window. His nephew arrives shortly—it is Charles Darnay, a name the young man assumed in England. The nephew and uncle are not on good terms. Darnay feels that the whole aristocracy is corrupt, that it places an unbearable burden on the French people. He announces that he will relinquish the family estate if he inherits it. His uncle feels that might makes right and intends to uphold his lordly privileges as long as he lives, even if it means imprisoning Darnay as a threat to the family honor. The Marquis is both polite and malevolent toward his nephew, wishing him dead after they part for the night. The next morning the nearby village is in a state of great turmoil: the Marquis St. Evrémonde has been murdered by a member of the Jacquerie.

A year later Charles Darnay is earning a good living in England by tutoring French, translating books, and writing about French literature. In love with Lucie Manette, he decides to ask her to marry him. However, he goes to see Dr. Manette first in order to get his consent. In talking with the doctor, Darnay reveals his love for Lucie but says it will never interfere with her love for her father. He asks the doctor not to prejudice Lucie against him, and after some hesitation Dr. Manette agrees. Then Darnay tries to tell the doctor of his past and his true identity, which upsets Manette considerably. The doctor stops him and makes him promise not to reveal the secret until the morning of the wedding. Darnay leaves, and later that night Lucie finds her father in a state of great agitation. He has reverted to his cobbling for an hour or so.

After finishing the session's legal work, Mr. Stryver announces to Sydney Carton that he intends to marry Lucie Manette, a girl whom he feels would make an admirable complement to a man of his position. Stryver assumes that he is eminently agreeable to women—tactful, ambitious, successful. He further assumes that Carton is particularly disagreeable to women and tells him so. Carton subtly jabs at Stryver's complacency, but Stryver cannot perceive Carton's satirical edge. Stryver aggressively continues his assault on Carton's faults and finally suggets that Carton find a wife from among the common people, with some property of her own, to take care of him in his declining years.

Stryver is on his way to the Manettes' home in Soho, and he stops in at Tellson's to inform Mr. Lorry of his plans for marriage. He is taken aback when Mr. Lorry hints that his suit will not be successful. Stryver angrily demands to know what could be wrong with himself as a prospective husband, and Mr. Lorry tells him that he may not be agreeable to Lucie. Stryver then accuses Lucie of being silly and giddy, an assertion that angers

Mr. Lorry. Nevertheless, Mr. Lorry advises him to wait while he himself goes to the Manette apartment to sound things out. Realizing he will be rejected, Stryver does an about-face; and when Mr. Lorry brings the expected news Stryver acts preoccupied and treats his proposal as an act of charity on his part that somehow misfired.

Shortly after the Stryver incident, Sydney Carton, who has been a frequent if moody visitor to the Manette apartment, drops in to speak to Lucie. Unusually sincere, Carton for once opens his heart to her, telling her that, while he will sink lower in life and while she can do nothing to prevent this fate, she has reawakened some of his old vitality and idealism. Initially uncomfortable with Carton, Lucie soon sheds tears of compassion for his wasted life. Carton tells her, finally, that should the occasion arise he would gladly sacrifice himself for her and anyone she loved.

Jerry Cruncher is sitting at his post outside Tellson's and watching the stream of traffic pass. He sees a hearse approach, and it is surrounded by a mob of people shouting, "Spies! Spies!" He learns that it is the funeral of Roger Cly, one of the police spies who testified against Darnay. The only mourner, threatened by the mob, makes a hasty escape. The mob decides to celebrate the occasion by going along to the graveyard, and Jerry Cruncher joins it. After the coffin is buried, the mob starts molesting passersby and looting shops. Cruncher, meanwhile, goes back alone, stopping at a surgeon's on the way.

At home that evening he accuses his wife of praying against him and threatens her. Once his wife and son are in bed, he goes out with a spade, crowbar, sack, and rope, and he is soon joined by two companions. His son, "Young Jerry," secretly follows him to the graveyard out of curiosity and watches him haul up the coffin. Young Jerry rushes home under the nightmare apprehension that the coffin is following him. He awakes the next morning to find his father beating his mother, assumes his father has had a luckless night, and cheers him up by telling him that he wants to be a "resurrection-man" (a body-snatcher) when he grows up.

Defarge's wineshop is full of men sullenly drinking one morning. Defarge arrives with a road mender, the same man who had told Darnay's uncle that he had seen a tall man riding under the carriage. A year has passed since that time, and Defarge takes the man up to Manette's old garret, where he tells the story of Gaspard, the Marquis' assassin, to the assembled Jacquerie. Gaspard, whose child was run down by the Marquis, murdered the Marquis for revenge and went into hiding for several months. Eventually he was captured, jailed, and hanged, and his corpse was left dangling by the village fountain, his very shadow poisoning the water and the town.

An initiate in the Jacquerie, the road mender is taken to Versailles one day, where he cheers the lords and ladies. Defarge approves of this because it will serve to make the courtiers more arrogant, which in turn will bring about their speedier destruction. Both Defarges think that the sight of these gaily dressed people will lead in time to the road mender's thirst for their blood.

On returning from Versailles the Defarges stop at a sentry box, where they learn of a new spy in their district, John Barsad. At the wineshop Defarge shows some weariness with the revolutionary activity, but his stern, determined wife advises him to be patient in the certainty that one day the Revolution will come. Defarge leaves for a few moments, and John Barsad drops in to sound the Defarges out. Madame Defarge adroitly parries his insinuations while knitting his name into her doomsday register. Defarge returns, and Barsad informs the two that Lucie Manette is about to marry Charles Darnay, the exiled member of the Evrémonde family. Madame Defarge then knits Darnay's name into the register as well. Her husband shows some surprise at the news. After Barsad leaves, Defarge expresses the hope that, for Lucie's sake, Darnay never returns to France. But his wife remains implacable.

Lucie Manette sets aside the night before her wedding to be alone with her father. Sitting in the courtyard, Lucie reassures her father that her love for Charles Darnay will not alter her love for him. Dr. Manette says he is happy with the impending marriage and expresses his fondness for Darnay, adding that one of his greatest apprehensions was that Lucie might somehow miss the joys of a husband and children. He goes on to mention his long imprisonment, when he did not know what happened to his unborn child and feared the child would grow up without knowing anything of him. For solace he imagined a daughter who would visit him in prison and lead him out of it at times; but he says that the happiness Lucie has brought him far exceeds the consolation of his old fancies. The two go in for dinner. Finally, Dr. Manette goes to bed, and Lucie returns later to sit by his bedside for a time.

Early the next morning Mr. Lorry arrives at the Manette home. While Dr. Manette has his promised interview with Darnay, Mr. Lorry wistfully thinks of himself as he might be if he had married, to which Miss Pross replies that he was born a bachelor. Dr. Manette emerges from the private interview visibly shaken. However, the wedding takes place, the doctor gives the bride away, and Lucie and Charles go off on a two-week honeymoon alone, after which Dr. Manette will join the newlyweds for a two-week trip through Wales. Mr. Lorry and Miss Pross see the doctor home. He is withdrawn, and a short time afterward they find him totally absorbed in his cobbling. Mr. Lorry decides to keep this a secret and takes a leave of absence from Tellson's to stay with Manette.

For nine days the cobbling continues, but on the tenth the doctor awakes fully recovered and unaware of what has happened in the interim. Mr. Lorry tactfully questions him on the morning of his recovery and learns that the recurrence of his old illness was due to some particularly painful recollection, that it is not likely to recur in the future, that it was not due to overwork, and that cobbling is merely the symptom of the illness, not its cause. In prison Dr. Manette took up cobbling to relieve his mental torment; it was a means of occupying himself. But for Lucie's sake the doctor agrees to surrender his cobbling tools and material. When he leaves to join the newlyweds on their trip Mr. Lorry and Miss Pross dismantle and dispose of the cobbling equipment.

Sydney Carton is the first to greet the Darnays on their return from the honeymoon. He takes Charles Darnay aside and tells him in an earnest tone that he feels guilty about the time after the trial when he was drunk and insulting to Darnay. He then asks permission, despite his general worthlessness, to be allowed to visit the family a few times a year. Darnay grants this request, and after Carton leaves he speaks of Carton in very

frank terms. However, on going to bed Lucie tells her husband
to be more considerate of Carton, who is an unfortunate man
with deep, seldom-revealed feelings.

Eight years later, in 1789, Lucie has had a daughter, who is
named after her, and a son who died young. Sydney Carton occasionally visits the Darnay family and is still working for Mr.
Stryver, who has married a prosperous window with three stupid
sons. Charles Darnay and Dr. Manette have been successful in
their work. But Lucie fancies that she will not live long. One
evening Mr. Lorry turns up in a cranky mood, having had to deal
at Tellson's with a flood of unexpected business from France;
and he recalls Lucie's old vision of the footsteps converging on
their lives.

Meanwhile, the citizens of Paris arm themselves. Led by
the Defarges, they storm the Bastille, slaughter its governor,
rescue seven prisoners (who are completely bewildered), and
impale the heads of seven guards on pikes. In the course of
storming the prison Defarge makes a thorough search of Dr.
Manette's old cell for some private reason of his own.

Back in Defarge's wineshop the revolutionists are celebrating this victory. Defarge comes in to announce that old Foulon,
a reactionary who told the people to eat grass, has been captured.
Foulon had given himself a mock burial to deceive the revolutionists, but the ruse did not work. Madame Defarge and her
aide, "The Vengeance," drum up a mob again to march on the
Hôtel de Ville, where Foulon is held captive. The mob, driven
to frenzy, dances through the streets, screaming for Foulon's
dismemberment. Foulon is tried and handed over to Madame
Defarge and the mob, who stuff his mouth with grass and hang
him from a lamp post, after which they behead him and put his
head on a pike. On learning that Foulon's son-in-law is riding
into Paris with troops, the mob also seizes him, putting his head
and heart on pikes. The people of Paris, seeing some hope of
change at last, celebrate their new power to destroy.

In the country village near the Evrémonde estate strangers
begin turning up. One rough fellow introduces himself to the
road mender as one of the Jacquerie, and they and two others
burn down the Evrémonde château by night. The villagers look
on in grim satisfaction and the officers of the prison stand by,

powerless in the face of this new spirit. Then the villagers threaten the house of Gabelle, the tax collector and Evrémonde steward. But Gabelle is saved by the dawn, which disperses the mob.

By 1792 Tellson's London office has become a center for the French emigrés. The Revolution in France has been triumphant, establishing its own government, confiscating property, and killing or jailing aristocrats who lacked the foresight to get out. Charles Darnay drops in at Tellson's and learns that Mr. Lorry is going to France on business. Despite much risk and inconvenience, Mr. Lorry intends to manage Tellson's Paris office and to salvage such property and secret papers as he can for its customers. Darnay is greatly disturbed by the events in France. Influenced by a letter pleading for help from Gabelle, who is in prison, by gibes from French exiles and from Stryver, and by Mr. Lorry's brave example, Darnay is tempted to return to his native country. He feels he has neglected his responsibilities in France. He also thinks he will be in no danger because he had voluntarily renounced his estate, which ought to secure him some influence with the new government and enable him to act as a force for mediation and mercy. He writes letters to his wife and father-in-law, which will be delivered after he has gone, and he leaves England without mentioning his plan to anyone.

Commentary

Dickens presents Tellson's as a parody of the Bastille in which men go in young and come out old, where secrets are hidden away, and where the physical features of the place are very similar to those of a prison. In fact, in a later chapter Dickens shows Mr. Lorry in Tellson's, and he is quite literally behind bars, which resemble the lines in a ledger. The nearness of Tellson's to Temple Bar, London's legal center, is not accidental, since it has contributed its share of heads to the ones that recently adorned Temple Bar. Tellson's is aligned with the Kingdom of Death, and to enter it one must descend two treacherous steps.

In discussing capital punishment in England Dickens indirectly amends his portrait of the country given in Chapter 1 of Book I. In effect, England's legal severity is almost as extreme as France's, yet this does nothing to reduce the number of crimes.

Dickens usually picks a character to serve as an index to the moral tone of a place, and in this chapter that character is Jerry Cruncher, the porter. Jerry Cruncher provides the main source of comic relief in a novel that is otherwise practically humorless; but the humor is "black comedy" based on brutality and a strange attitude toward prayer. Cruncher embodies in a comic way two principal themes of the novel (which will be discussed later). Dickens gradually reveals clues about him that point to some mystery, like his antagonism to prayer, his boots muddied during the night, his insistence on his view of himself as "an honest tradesman," his sleepless eyes, his hoarseness, the rust on his fingers, his fear of ghosts. He is conceived in his entirety from the first, a remarkable feat for a novelist writing installments for weekly publication in a magazine. Nowhere in this novel is Dickens' craftsmanship as expert as it is in this relatively minor character.

Dickens had a penchant for creating passive, suffering protagonists, men and women whose virtue and grace consist in bearing up under intolerable circumstances. This very passivity accounts for the lifelessness of Charles Darnay and Lucie Manette. The flaw lies in Dickens' conception of virtue as an inactive quality, akin to the Calvinist notion of "grace" as something God-given and unattainable by good works. Passive virtue is undramatic and therefore unsusceptible to Dickens' ability to create vivid characters. When Dickens' heroes or heroines are given a dramatic scene, as in Lucie's exhortation to her father in Book I, Chapter 6, the result is often dreadfully sentimental.

Darnay, like Dr. Manette, has to be rescued from the Kingdom of Death. They are both victims of an oppressive social machinery, and as victims are unable to secure their own release. Here is the theme of resurrection again, of being "recalled to life." Ironically, this time Lucie and Mr. Lorry are accomplices of the forces of death. But the finest irony comes when Darnay falls in love with Lucie just as she is producing the most damaging circumstantial evidence against him. The fact that she remembers every detail of their encounter five years back and her evident anxiety for him presumably carry more weight with him.

Dickens, by pairing Mr. Lorry off in conversation with Miss Pross, subtly calls attention to each one's unmarried status. This is important because each of them is a protective figure to the

Manettes, having no families of their own. In a sense they are like a fairy godmother and fairy godfather. Miss Pross, in fact, seems to have almost occult powers as a cook, being able to produce delicious meals from the most unpromising ingredients.

Despite the uneasy tensions of the gathering, Dickens' basic impulse is to create an idyll of the setting in Soho, a place of quiet friendship away from the turmoil of politics. However, the real source of the idyll lies in the affection of everyone present for Lucie Manette. She is "the golden thread" of Book II, the incarnation of concern and compassion. Characteristically, her fainting fits arise from her anxiety about someone else, notably her father and Darnay. In her purity she is given the role of prophetess, vaguely apprehending the role of the French Revolution in the future of the group. Yet one feels that perhaps Dickens is placing too much weight on such an unrealized character.

Dickens' methods here are not very far from those of Perrault, the French author of fairy tales. Dickens consciously plays up these traits by suggesting that Monseigneur, on retiring to his chamber, is secreted away by chocolate sprites; or by drawing a parallel between the carriage whips and snakes, as an incarnation of the Furies; or by likening Darnay's uncle to a tigerish sorcerer in the act of transforming himself. Of course, the Marquis St. Evrémonde is akin to the wicked uncle of folklore who wrests away his nephew's inheritance. (Ironically, it is the nephew who renounces the estate.) Evrémonde naturally lives in a sinister château that looks "as if the Gorgon's head had surveyed it."

However, this technique does not detract from the hallucinatory brilliance of these chapters. The suite of Monseigneur is a kind of Satanic temple, and he is like a Satanic priest receiving an unholy eucharist of chocolate before leaving his "Holy of Holies." Appropriately, the atmosphere in his suite is disfigured by "the leprosy of unreality," where no one is what he pretends to be, where everyone is skeptical, and where boredom and uselessness are fashionable. This whole aristocratic society places an extreme emphasis on external traits and pretenses. It is always dressed as if for a fancy ball. And even the hangman is exquisitely dressed, Dickens tells us; the lowest official occupation is used here as an index to the style of the era. Dickens has the insight to see that this emphasis on external show masks an inward emptiness, that it is an attempt to deny the existence of death. The fancy ball flashing through the streets of Paris in costly carriages is really a *danse macabre*.

A further point should be made about Monseigneur: he is one big digestive tract, swallowing France's resources as he swallows his chocolate. Dickens uses him to embody selfish privilege. His digestive system is the only living thing about him: it has usurped all of his reality until he has become a kind of human snake.

Animal images crop up frequently in this section. The people, gaunt and superficially submissive, are viewed as rats, pigs, dogs, and vermin by Darnay's uncle, who in turn is seen as a tiger. Thus, in denying the humanity of the poor he has become subhuman and beastly himself.

Dickens makes symbolic use of a geographical detail in placing the Cathedral of Notre Dame equidistant between Monseigneur's suite and the slums. It is as if he is weighing the aristocracy against the poor with the cathedral as the fulcrum of the scales. Notre Dame is symbolic here of both God's judgment and Christian principles. These latter are the standards Dickens uses throughout the novel to judge the acts of his characters. Dickens has nothing but scorn for the high-handed behavior of his aristocrats, for their lack of faith, their selfishness and unreality. They are purposely as stylized and petrified as the stone heads that decorate the Evrémonde château (another detail that anticipates the beheadings of the French Revolution). In fact, after the Marquis St. Evrémonde's murder one of those same stone heads seems to take on his physical features.

These chapters portray Darnay, Stryver, and Carton as suitors for Lucie Manette's hand, although Carton knows his suit is hopeless and declines to propose. In the simplest terms, Lucie's choice is between a handsome and hardworking young man, a gross, portly boor, and a wasted alcoholic. The outcome, therefore, is scarcely in doubt. Yet Dickens makes this section interesting by creating a mysterious tension between Darnay and Dr. Manette, and by showing the different approach each uses. Darnay tactfully appeals to the person closest to Lucie before proposing and reassures him that he does not intend to separate Lucie from her father. On the contrary, Darnay says he intends to knit the family ties even closer together. Stryver boast-fully divulges his marriage plans to Carton in a scene that parodies Darnay's conversation with Dr. Manette. And he is about to shoulder his way into the Manette home when Mr. Lorry cautions him. Learning that his suit is futile, Stryver immediate-ly contrives to put Lucie in the wrong. While Carton is not, strictly speaking, a suitor, he still makes a partial claim on Lucie's heart. The scene between him and Lucie is genuinely moving, even if much of Carton's talk is based on self-pity.

Darnay's interview with Dr. Manette hints at some secret of which Manette is aware and which is very painful to him. The reader begins to suspect that it has to do with some wrong perpetrated by Darnay's family, which involves Dr. Manette's imprisonment. Sensing this, one sees there is a very real reason for this interview; that Dr. Manette could easily ruin Darnay's marriage plans if he chose to. All that Darnay realizes at this point is that Dr. Manette occasionally looks at him with dislike and fear, and that there is some undisclosed reason behind the doctor's uneasiness.

In Stryver's conversation with Carton it is plain that Stryver is a pompous, self-satisfied, insensitive, obnoxious man. He speaks in monologue, talking not *to* Carton but *at* him. He seems much more concerned with his own public image than with Carton's sensibilities. His most active physical part is his shoulder, which he figuratively uses to wedge his way up in the world while "shouldering out" weaker men like Carton. Stryver regards Lucie as a prospective appendage to his own greatness, as an acquisition not much different from a piece of furniture. Darnay and Carton feel love for Lucie, but Stryver's motives are essentially material and selfish, arising from his need to ap-propriate things. At Tellson's he tends to swell up, to take over all the available room, as if his body were mimicking his inflated self-importance. And his complacency is unpuncturable: re-jected by Lucie, he immediately makes her out to be a fool. This single-minded devotion to his self-esteem betrays a vanity and self-interest that are appalling, but Dickens keeps the tone satirical: after Mr. Lorry brings Stryver the news and gets shoved out, Stryver lies down on his couch and blinks at the ceiling in disbelief.

Carton's interest in Lucie does not seem to be sensual. He is not going to marry her or reform himself, but she has renewed his old idealism, inspiring in him an urge for self-sacrifice. Carton appears to be a social and emotional failure, partly owing to his heavy drinking, but he has the power to work on Lucie's feelings. His style is either flippantly caustic or intensely sincere, with no tonal range in between. Lucie calls forth his sincerity, and Carton seems to value her compassion above anything else. This relationship is limited and pure, just as Stryver's is limited and selfish. Only Darnay has the power to inspire Lucie's love. And one feels that these two pallid characters deserve each other.

One notable thing about Jerry Cruncher is his use of euphemisms, a common feature of lower-middle-class life. But with him they take an interesting twist. He refers to himself as an "honest tradesman," a comic pretension to respectability, and to his body-snatching as "fishing." The queerest euphemism he uses is "flopping," by which he means prayer. It is as if he inverts normal values by finding an impolite term for a respectable practice and by finding polite expressions for his questionable work. The humor of this gets rather thin and mechanical after a while, but it is related to the central concerns of the novel.

The fact that Jerry Cruncher beats his wife for praying the morning after his expedition to the graveyard suggests that something went wrong, a fact that will be confirmed later. The alert reader may have guessed that the single mourner who ran off was John Barsad, Cly's accomplice at the Darnay trial, and will be prepared for a reappearance of the police spy in a later chapter.

Madame Defarge is the revolutionary impulse incarnate, the central character of this section. If Lucie Manette is the center of the group in the London suburb of Soho, Madame Defarge is the center of the revolutionaries in the Paris suburb of St. Antoine. Each is passive, yet Lucie's group is bound by love while Madame Defarge's is held together by class-hatred. Stony, absorbed in her constant knitting, seemingly unobservant, Madame Defarge is in absolute control of these people. With her indomitable will she seems less a person than a force of destiny. As in his portrayal of the French aristocrats, who embody abstract Privilege, Dickens tends to reveal Madame Defarge as an allegorical figure of Fate. And in the final paragraphs of Chapter 16 Dickens multiplies her into hundreds of knitting women, a revolutionary society that knits to keep the mind off hunger, and which will knit at the foot of the guillotine.

Although the action of this section takes place in 1781, a good eight years before the Revolution, Dickens presents the Revolution as an inevitability. He is writing in the hindsight of accomplished fact, which of course does violence to the way things really happen. The Revolution possibly might have been avoided in actuality, but Dickens never entertains this idea. His abstract manner of conceiving things shows the Revolution to be foreordained, a social expiation for an overwhelming injustice. Dickens' fictional world, in fact, is semi-mechanical. Everything is interrelated; coincidence is really the working out of a moral logic; and some immutable law determines the destiny of his characters according to their deserving, with good rewarded and evil punished. Still, it is an author's privilege to imitate God, to create a world that is true for himself — a world modeled on some ideological conception that gives it coherence. Despite the appearance of accident in Dickens' plotting, like Barsad turning up as a spy in Paris, this novel is free of chance, and is therefore neatly and perfectly modeled. The Revolution is not, for Dickens, a political inevitability but a moral one, and is absolutely necessary to Dickens' scheme of things.

In the conversation between Dr. Manette and Mr. Lorry both men refer to the doctor in the third person, as if he were someone else. This is a subtle tribute to his being divorced from himself, to his steadfast refusal to face his tormented half. And the tormented self, in return, has converted him for a time into a mindless automaton that is utterly cut off from the world. Moreover, in a later breakdown of this same kind Dickens explicitly refers to Dr. Manette as "it."

His cobbling has a counterpart in Madame Defarge's knitting. Both occupations suggest a form of revenge on the world in Dickens' presentation. Both are wholly absorbing activities, in Manette's case to keep his mind off his torment, and in the case of Madame Defarge and her knitting, to keep the mind off hunger. While cobbling and knitting are useful activities, Dickens gives them a sinister aspect. When asked what she is knitting at

Versailles, Madame Defarge replies, "Shrouds," and knits out the names of people she intends to have killed in the coming Revolution. Dr. Manette, on the other hand, creates shoes for imaginary people, and since the pair on which he has been working is for a young woman, one infers from the context that he is making shoes for his imaginary prison daughter, as if when his actual daughter leaves for a while he must turn to his prison hallucination for comfort.

Dickens cannot really delineate a convincing relationship between a couple. The scene between Lucie and Darnay in their bedroom is terribly stilted. Darnay's endearments — "my own," "my Life," "dear Heart" — are chillingly formal and melodramatic; and Lucie's speech is no better. Dickens lacks any sense of fun between lovers: a tone of frigid earnestness kills any playfulness between his couples, something one notices with the Defarges as well. This is partly due to Victorian prudery, but it also stems from Dickens' view of women, who in his world are either pure or corrupt, with few alternatives between the pedestal and the gutter. Women are not viewed as men's equals, an attitude common in Victorian times. Dicken's contemporaries may have found this bedroom scene true to life because they probably shared Dickens' premises.

Events are rapidly speeded up. Dickens deals with eight years of married life, the progress of the characters in England, and the storming of the Bastille in Paris, all in one chapter. Much of the prose in narrating the events in the Darnay family life is undistinguished and sugary, but when Dickens switches in mid-chapter to the mob's assault on the Bastille his prose jumps to life with a fierce, masculine energy. Domestic life, it seems, has become much less interesting to Dickens (and to the reader) than public affairs in France. Despite the foolhardiness of Darnay's plan to return to France, one sympathizes with the decision.

The difficulty with idylls, of course, is that they are static. They represent a harbor of peace in an anxious world. But Dickens introduces some unsettling elements into the Soho idyll. Mr. Lorry is presented as old and crotchety after eight years, and only the prospect of going to France restores a measure of youthfulness to him. The Darnay's only son dies as a young boy,

and Lucie fears she also will die soon. Later we see Darnay finding many reasons why he should go to France. Presumably he is
going to rescue Gabelle, a man he has not seen in twelve years,
but he also imagines he can play a beneficial role in the Revolution. It is as if a daughter, friends, and conjugal love were inadequate for the Darnays' happiness. Darnay thinks he will find
his destiny in France — a spiritual estate, so to speak, in return
for the material estate that he relinquished.

Darnay by this time is thirty-seven, and he seems to have
some thought in mind of recapturing the spirit of his youth. In
fact, he refers to Mr. Lorry's youthfulness several times, as if he
secretly had a middle-aged envy of the youthful attitude. Dickens himself had separated from his wife a year before he wrote
this book, and it is certain that he knew the dissatisfactions of
middle age. Be that as it may, the prose, when it returns to Darnay in Chapter 24, appears to lose some of its dynamism. The
rather static quality of the idyll in Soho is underlined by the
uninspired, often sentimental style that Dickens uses to portray
it. What makes this so evident is the tumult of the events in
France, which is emphasized by an exciting and dramatic prose.
After two and a half chapters dealing with the uprisings in
France, we realize the foolishness of Darnay's return. Madame
Defarge, we know, already has his name in her doomsday register. Darnay seems to be blundering into a situation in which
death is almost certain.

Dickens shows that mob rule exists in France, and the mobs
are particularly bloodthirsty. Within a few hours the mob that
was purposeful and effective in storming the Bastille becomes
a howling, breast-beating band of demons. Dickens refers to the
revolutionary mobs as a sea time and again. This metaphor refers to the mob's pounding, surging, destructive force, to its
amorphousness, its unity, and its unfeelingness. Flush with the
triumph of the Bastille, the mob feels itself to be omnipotent and
invulnerable. After the storming of the prison, Madame
Defarge's first act is to order the beheading of its governor, and
then a good many decapitations ensue.

Madame Defarge can be seen as a lower-class version of
Darnay's uncle, despite the differences of sex and their mutual
class-hatred. What is polished and deliberate cruelty in the

Marquis becomes in her a cruelty hidden by impassiveness; both are unrelenting in their purposes, both are self-absorbed. Madame Defarge, in her efforts to revenge herself on the aristocracy, has assimilated some of its traits.

BOOK III

Summary

Charles Darnay finds the journey to Paris in 1792 very inconvenient and bothersome, taking longer than he had anticipated. This is because of the lack of adequate facilities for transportation and the officiousness of the local Revolutionary authorities. Darnay realizes that retreat is impossible and that he must go on to Paris to obtain official clearance. At one village he is awakened in the night and given two escorts, since he is an aristocrat. Farther on, at Beauvais, he is mobbed by an angry crowd, but the quick thinking of one of his escorts saves him. There he learns that all emigrant property has been confiscated by the new Republic. Arriving at the gates of Paris, he is interrogated by Defarge, who tells him that he has no rights and that he is to be jailed "in secret." Defarge leads him to the prison of La Force, where he is imprisoned briefly with pallid, ghostlike members of the gentility, who treat him with sympathy and courtesy. Later he is taken to a private cell, where ominous, familiar phantom voices plague him.

A few days later Mr. Lorry is sitting in Tellson's elegant Paris office, and he is anxious and depressed. A grindstone has been placed in the courtyard outside, and some terrible event is about to take place. Mr. Lorry answers the doorbell to find Lucie and Dr. Manette, who tell him that they have come because of Charles. They have learned he is imprisoned at La Force, a piece of news that terrifies Mr. Lorry. He sends Lucie into another room and informs Dr. Manette that the mob now outside the window, sharpening its knives and weapons on the grindstone, is butchering the prisoners at La Force. As a former inmate of the Bastille, Dr. Manette has some influence with the revolutionaries, so he leaves to try to save Darnay from being killed. On returning to Lucie, Mr. Lorry finds Miss Pross and young Lucie with her, and he allows them to stay for the night.

Mr. Lorry, as a businessman, fears he will endanger Tellson's if he allows Darnay's family to stay longer. He finds an apartment for them in an inconspicuous place and leaves his bodyguard, Jerry Cruncher, to watch over them. Mr. Lorry soon receives a message from Dr. Manette, delivered by Defarge, that Darnay is safe for the time being. Defarge also carries a note to Lucie from her husband. He asks to be taken to her, along with Madame Defarge and "The Vengeance," presumably so they can identify and protect her. The message delivered, Lucie implores Madame Defarge to do what she can for Darnay. But Madame Defarge brushes off the entreaty and takes a sinister interest in young Lucie, casting a literal and figurative shadow on both Lucie and her daughter.

Dr. Manette returns to Mr. Lorry in four days and tells him of the horrors of the mob's executions and of how he interceded for his son-in-law before the prison tribunal. While he failed to get Darnay freed, he managed to keep him safe in prison and away from the mob. He tells Mr. Lorry that, for Lucie's sake, he will do everything in his power to save Darnay. As a physician Dr. Manette has access to the prisons, and because of his personal prestige as a former prisoner in the Bastille he can convey messages between Darnay and Lucie. However, because of a fresh outbreak of revolutionary fervor he is unable to obtain Darnay's trial or release for a year and three months.

Meanwhile, Lucie, having set up housekeeping in Paris, is full of worry. She goes to the prison each day and stands outside on the chance that her husband will see her. But her spot is right beside a wood-sawyer's shop. The wood-sawyer, once the road mender, is a jovial, malicious man who threatens her into giving him drinking money. One December day Lucie sees a dancing, howling, clapping mob come whirling by, performing the wild Revolutionary dance, the Carmagnole; and when it passes she finds her father standing protectively over her. He says that it is all right to signal to Darnay this time, and just as she does so Madame Defarge walks by. Her father also tells her that Darnay's trial will be the following day. Together they go to inform Mr. Lorry, who is with an unidentified man.

Darnay is summoned before the Tribunal and defends himself ably in front of a rascally jury. He says he gave up his inheritance and went to live in England, where he earned his own living, in order to avoid oppressing the French people by an expensive, useless existence. He returned to France to save an old family servant, Gabelle, who had just been released a few days before this trial because the Republic had captured Darnay. However, Dr. Manette's testimony on Darnay's behalf sways the jury, which acquits him.

The crowd in the courtroom swarms over Darnay with hugging, kissing, and tears. He is carried home by the mob and is rather apprehensive. The mob breaks into the frenzied Carmagnole. Lucie faints, then celebrates her husband's release by praying. Finally, she thanks her father for his great service in saving Darnay.

Dr. Manette is pleased with his achievement the evening after the trial, but Lucie is still apprehensive about her husband's safety. Miss Pross asks if they will be leaving France soon, and the doctor replies that it is not safe yet. Miss Pross then leaves with Jerry Cruncher on a shopping expedition. Lucie and her father hear a knock at the door and find four men there to arrest Darnay on new charges. Darnay has been accused by the Defarges and one other person, and his new trial will take place the next day. Stunned, the doctor asks who the third accuser is, but the surprised guard refuses to answer.

Miss Pross and Jerry Cruncher enter a wineshop, where both are startled by the sight of a man who is about to leave. Miss Pross recognizes him as her brother, Solomon Pross, and Cruncher remembers him from Darnay's trial in England. It is the man known as John Barsad. Frightened by these recognitions, Barsad tells them to keep quiet and step outside. Then the three are joined by Sydney Carton, who recently arrived in Paris. Carton knows Barsad to be a prison informer and coerces him into going to Tellson's, taking Cruncher along too.

At Tellson's Carton informs Mr. Lorry that Darnay has been arrested again, and that Dr. Manette was helpless to prevent it. Carton then turns to Barsad and proceeds to intimidate him. Barsad, as a former English spy, might still be in the pay of the English government. Furthermore, as an associate of Roger Cly, who is now in France and working as an informer, Barsad would be a likely candidate for the guillotine. Jerry Cruncher, meanwhile, has vouched for the fact that Cly's burial in England twelve years back was a ruse. With Jerry Cruncher and Mr. Lorry as witnesses, Barsad is compelled to ask what Carton wants. Carton asks if he has access to the prison. Barsad says he does, and Carton leads him into another room.

While Carton and Barsad have their conference, Mr. Lorry warns Jerry Cruncher that he will be discharged back in England for carrying on body-snatching under the cover of his job at Tellson's. Cruncher replies that respectable clients are implicated too — surgeons, undertakers, sextons — and that if he is discharged it will only drive him into body-snatching as a regular occupation, and he is already sick of corpses from witnessing the Revolution. Mr. Lorry relents on the condition that Cruncher will not resume his clandestine employment.

Carton and Barsad emerge from the other room, their business concluded, and Barsad and Cruncher leave. Carton tells Mr. Lorry that the best he can do is to secure access to Darnay in his cell, which causes Mr. Lorry to weep. Carton is moved by Mr. Lorry's tears and reminds him that he has led a useful, warm-hearted life, that Lucie and her daughter will mourn him when he dies, and that the worst thing in life is to die unmourned. Mr. Lorry leaves Tellson's to comfort Lucie and her father. Carton walks the streets all night, tracing Lucie's path to the prison, with the biblical passage, "I am the resurrection and the life,..." echoing in his mind. And at one point he drops in at a chemist's shop to make a purchase.

The next day Carton attends Darnay's new trial. The jury is composed of rowdy, vicious people. The Defarges are cited as Darnay's accusers, but so is Dr. Manette! Defarge had retrieved some hidden papers from the doctor's old cell when the Bastille was stormed; and on the evidence of these papers Darnay is accused of being the last of a long line of evil aristocrats. Everyone listens intently as the manuscript is read.

In 1757 Dr. Manette was commanded by the Evrémonde twins to accompany them in secret to a country house outside of Paris. There he found a delirious young woman and her dying brother, both victims of the younger twin. From the dying young man he learned that the Evrémondes had caused the death of the whole family, except for a younger sister who had been removed to safety. The young man laid a blood curse on the Evrémondes and then died; and his delirious, ravished sister died shortly afterward.

The Evrémonde twins were uneasy about the doctor and his reluctance to accept payment. Dr. Manette decided to write a letter reporting the incident to the Court. But before he posted it he was visited by the older twin's wife and her son, who was about two or three years old at the time. She had learned of the story and wanted to make secret amends to the missing younger sister. The doctor could not help her, so she told her young son (Charles Darnay) to pledge himself to righting the wrong committed by his uncle and father. Manette then posted the letter; and a few days later he was taken from his pregnant wife and jailed in secret by the Evrémondes, who had intercepted his letter.

After the reading of the manuscript is finished Madame Defarge gloats over her triumph and tells the doctor to save his son-in-law if he can. The jury, under the impact of the tale, votes for Darnay's death as the last of the Evrémondes.

Having been present throughout the trial, Lucie Darnay is horrified by the sentence on her husband. The crowd leaves, and she asks permission from the guards to kiss her husband for the last time, which is granted. She tries to comfort Darnay and remarks that she will soon join him in Heaven. Dr. Manette approaches the couple, and Darnay tells him that he has done nothing to reproach himself for, having done all that was humanly possible on their behalf. But all the doctor can do is give a shriek of anguish. Charles is led back to prison with his execution set for the next day. When Lucie faints at her father's feet, Sydney Carton springs forward and lifts her into a carriage, which Manette and Mr. Lorry also enter, and the group goes to Lucie's apartment. There, although knowing the case to be hopeless, Carton urges Dr. Manette to see if he can use his personal influence again as a last resort. After kissing Lucie, who is still unconscious, Carton leaves.

Knowing his close resemblance to Darnay, Carton decides to make himself known and so he goes to the Defarge wineshop. The Defarges, having noticed the similarity and thinking Carton no more than an Englishman with little knowledge of French, proceed to argue in his presence over the question of whether

Lucie and her father and child should be guillotined too. Madame Defarge thinks they should because she herself was the youngest daughter of the injured family, but her husband is for drawing the line at Darnay. Carton, of course, overhears the quarrel and goes to tell Mr. Lorry to have a carriage and everyone's passport ready at two o'clock the following day. In the meantime Dr. Manette has returned from his fruitless mission in a demented state and asks for his cobbling equipment.

Back in prison on the eve of his execution, Charles Darnay slowly composes himself. He writes letters to his wife, his father-in-law, and Mr. Lorry in which he commends each to the others' care. He sleeps that night and wakes the next morning with a new preoccupation—the exact manner in which his execution will take place. Time passes slowly, but at one o'clock Sydney Carton enters the cell, forces him to exchange clothes, gets him to write a brief note to Lucie (which Carton dictates), and drugs him until he is unconscious. Darney is then carried off by Barsad and some guards to be placed in Mr. Lorry's carriage. Carton, having put on Darnay's clothes, is summoned by the guards at two, in his role as Charles Darnay. He is led to the room where the prisoners wait to be taken to the guillotine. His imposture is recognized by a meek little seamstress, and she asks Carton to hold her hand on the way to the guillotine.

In the carriage Mr. Lorry presents the passports at the gates of Paris and he identifies the passengers: Dr. Manette, Lucie and her daughter, Sydney Carton (who is really Darnay), and himself. The passports are accepted, and the group, despite many anxious delays, makes its escape from France.

In secret conference with some of her companions, Madame Defarge announces that she will inform on Lucie and her daughter that evening, after Darnay's beheading. Then she leaves for Lucie's apartment, thinking to find Lucie upset and ready to say treasonable things.

Meanwhile, Miss Pross has been left behind with Jerry Cruncher to expedite the escape. They make preparations to leave. Miss Pross tells Jerry Cruncher to wait for her with the carriage outside Notre Dame cathedral. Cruncher vows to stop body-snatching and beating his wife for praying if Mr. Lorry and his group make it safely back to England.

Madame Defarge finds Miss Pross alone in the apartment, and she demands to know where Lucie is. Unable to understand her, Miss Pross at least grasps her threatening intentions and backs protectively against a closed door. Madame Defarge then tries to enter that room and grapples with Miss Pross, who is her equal in strength. In pulling a pistol from her bosom Madame Defarge is shot and killed. Miss Pross is permanently deafened by the blast. After locking the apartment, she rushes to meet Jerry Cruncher, and together they escape.

The tumbrils rolling through the streets of Paris are the inevitable result of overbearing privilege and an oppressed people, Dickens says. Sydney Carton in his tumbril ignores the screaming crowds, notices Barsad looking at him fearfully, but concentrates on comforting the seamstress. They kiss before she ascends the guillotine, and then he follows her in a tranquil and triumphant mood.

Before he dies Sydney Carton has a vision in which the principal revolutionists in the novel follow him to the guillotine; the evil gradually wears itself out and a happier, more secure period follows. He envisions, too, his own survival in the memories of the Darnay family, who will name a son after him. The son will become a just and successful judge, thereby fulfilling Carton's own thwarted ambitions.

Commentary

The movement of the first chapter consists of Darnay's journey to Paris, which is both a physical and spiritual ordeal. This is a journey to the center of the Kingdom of Death, and it ends in a damp, solitary cell. Every step of the journey entails some new threat, some new loss of freedom, as his hope of retreat is ended and the menace of the revolutionists becomes larger and more real. Along the route Darnay sees rude interference, charred ruins, people dancing and singing in the middle of the night, a mob about to attack him. At Paris he finds that his rights have been abrogated, and that he is no more than a cipher in the new political order. He seems worse off than the living ghosts of the old order that he meets in prison because he has been jailed "in secret." The social hierarchy has been turned topsy-turvy: mobs flourish while respectability languishes in prison.

We hear echoes of Dr. Manette in the background. At Beauvais, the doctor's old village, a mob tries to kill Darnay. At Paris, Darnay is questioned by Defarge, whom we know is Manette's old servant, but who will do nothing for Darnay. And when he is brought to his solitary cell we remember that the doctor, too, had been jailed in such a place—a fact emphasized by ghostly voices saying, "he made shoes, he made shoes." These echoes suggest that Dr. Manette's experience is being repeated here.

Here we see Dr. Manette's heroism in rescuing Darnay from mob execution and from the threat of the guillotine. He also works tirelessly as a doctor for over a year in attempting to have Darnay brought to trial, where he can use his influence. But this is the limit of his positive authority.

His motive in restoring Lucie's husband to her is to repay her for her service in restoring him, a payment in kind that brings out his masculine pride in assuming the role of head of the family to Lucie and Darnay, who are necessarily dependent on him. He is also a charismatic figure to the mobs, who respect him. And his old servant, Defarge, seems to regard him as a sort of father.

One realizes that Darnay came to France in a futile attempt to save a man's life and win influence with the revolutionists in order to do good; but here we see Dr. Manette doing precisely this, while Darnay languishes in jail. It seems to be Darnay's fate to undertake some noble venture that fails, leaving others to rescue him from his predicament.

Dickens here creates three mob scenes, which elaborate on the mob scenes in Book II. The first, in which the mob slaughters the prisoners at La Force, is a companion piece to the storming of the Bastille. There the mob breaks into prison to free the captives; here it butchers them. In Book II the Bastille represents the law and social coercion. But La Force represents a literal revolution of moral and social values; it stands for mob government and anarchy. The prisoners at La Force stand for the established hierarchy of values—for virtue, beauty, intelligence, wealth, polish, respectability. And the mob stands for the lowest common human denominator, for a bestial murderousness that uses its power to destroy all that is exceptional or worthy.

In the second mob scene, the Carmagnole that Lucie sees, we recognize the dance of the mob that marches on the Hôtel de

Ville in Book II. But the dance now has an official function, it has been ritualized. Dancing has become a perversion of itself. It is not an act of joy, but one of frenzy, and it is used to steel its participants to bloodshed. The dance itself, which is captured by Dickens in a quick, rhapsodic prose, expresses by its very intensity a will toward destruction and self-destruction.

In the third mob scene, after the trial, the crowd that rushes to congratulate Darnay would have torn him to pieces in different circumstances. On the way home, carried by the mob, Darnay thinks for a moment he is in a tumbril. This mob, having come to the courtroom to see men condemned to death, ends by celebrating with the Carmagnole, thereby combining the functions of the other two mobs.

The slogan of the Republic, "Liberty, Equality, Fraternity, or Death," is equivocal. It means to say that one can choose one or the other, but it can also be taken as an equation. Dickens uses Samson, the executioner, to summarize the revolutionary fervor and its corruption. He is figuratively the national hangman of Chapter 7 of Book II stripped of his finery and set to work in earnest.

That the mob is Satanic goes without saying. Its members have discarded the crosses around their necks for miniature guillotines. Moreover, the mob has unofficially canonized that instrument, referring to it as "Sainte Guillotine," the symbol of the new Republic. Even the Cathedral of Notre Dame must fly the black flag of this new government. Like Satan, the mob leaves its mark everywhere. But these are superficial items. The real diabolism of the mob rests in its overweening arrogance, its godlike assumption of power over the lives of everyone in France. The mob's occasional acts of generosity merely serve to show its power.

In this climate Lucie is a lost, anxious creature, and she is in great need of protection. She meets Madame Defarge twice in these chapters, and each time the impending menace of the latter is emphasized. Madame Defarge's power is still latent and unrevealed, which adds to her sinister aura. But Dr. Manette has expended all of his positive power. Threatening forces seem to concentrate on Lucie, possibly because in her weakness she is most vulnerable to them; she could lose her whole family.

The wood-sawyer points this out by illustrating with his saw how the heads of Lucie, her husband, and their daughter would tumble from the guillotine.

Darnay's trial invites some comparisons with his trial in England thirteen years before. The issue again is treason, not treason of deed but treason of status — the treason of being an aristocrat in a republic. Further, emigrés are by definition traitors in the new order; and back in England, Darnay was accused of treason because of his frequent trips to France. So his dual nationality has brought him under suspicion twice. Darnay's motive each time is that he was on an errand of mercy; in the first instance to redress some family wrong, and in the second to save the family steward. Only the family honor, it appears, can put him in jeopardy, but the risk is always a total one which involves his very life. And his loved ones now share the same risk.

This section deals with three kinds of power, which is embodied in these three contestants. Dr. Manette's power is shown in Chapter 7 to derive from masculine pride in reasserting himself as the head of the family. He takes pleasure in the dependence of Lucie and Darnay on him after his own long dependence on them. Madame Defarge humiliates that pride and renders him powerless by confronting him with his old tortured prison self through Defarge's reading of the manuscript. Dr. Manette's secret self remains dormant until it has a chance to take over completely; Manette's power stems from his successful struggle against this internal opponent. But because he is divided against himself and because his male pride arises from his conscious self-victory, he is always vulnerable to the exposure of his tormented self. The reader, therefore, can anticipate his total collapse after this new trial.

Madame Defarge's power derives from her secret but all-engrossing lust for vengeance on the Evrémonde family, an urge that has stored up its potency through long years of malevolent brooding. One realizes how she has managed the action behind the scenes by letting Dr. Manette expend his force in a mock victory, accusing Darnay again, bringing him to a new trial, and using Dr. Manette's own manuscript to secure Darnay's condemnation. However, she remains in the background until Darnay's death sentence is virtually assured, and then she bursts forth in a gibe at the doctor's defeat. The reader may anticipate the fact that she is the missing younger sister of the young man who laid his dying curse on the Evrémondes. Ironically, in being sentenced to death, Darnay both fulfills his pledge to his mother to make restitution to the missing sister and fulfills the blood curse on his family.

Sydney Carton's power also has its source in a long-hidden secret—his intense, hopeless love for Lucie Darnay, which has prepared itself for an ultimate act of self-sacrifice. And, like Madame Defarge, Sydney Carton works secretly, although the reader can easily guess his intentions. There is the implicit irony that love will take Carton precisely to where his dissipation was leading him—an early death. Madame Defarge, with her power of hate, has almost expended her force, just as Dr. Manette had earlier. From now on the novel will be Carton's, and his power of love will triumph.

Alongside this major action several minor things take place which are worth examining. In Chapter 8 the ubiquitous Roger Cly turns up, after his mock funeral in England twelve years before. Again, the forces of evil must parody the resurrection theme, playing out a false death followed by a false rebirth. Unlike old Foulon, who also had a mock burial, Cly can side with any power, whether reactionary or revolutionary; he is a spy without allegiance. Cly and Barsad are companion spirits who are willing to earn a little money by creating misery no matter what the cause or place—a pair of evil chameleons that take on the coloration of their surroundings.

In blackmailing Barsad, Carton treats the matter like a casual game of cards, producing his threats as one would lay cards on the table, and he wins the game. Barsad is forced to comply. But immediately after this scene Mr. Lorry parodies Carton's action by blackmailing Jerry Cruncher into giving up body-snatching by threatening to fire him. Thus, good men sometimes use underhanded means to achieve good purposes.

Dickens then changes the mood to one of sentiment in treating Carton's conversation with Mr. Lorry and his long night walk. Despite some sentimentality in this part, the reader is moved because he has guessed what Carton is planning. The repetition of the passage from John 11:25-26, and the brief scene when

Carton carries a little girl across the street and asks her for a kiss, add to a genuine feeling of compassion for the man. Almost in spite of Dickens at times we realize that Carton is one of the redeemed.

He seems cast as a Christian knight now, holding his night-long vigil in a place of peril, sustained by the image of Lucie, whom he loves purely. That Lucie is married to Darnay does not hinder him, just as it did not hinder courtly lovers in the Middle Ages. In his devotion to her Carton traces her path through the Valley of the Shadow, with the prison on one side and the murderous wood-sawyer on the other. And during his night walk Carton buys a mysterious potion.

The manuscript of Dr. Manette, which Defarge reads at the trial, is practically a compilation of all the Romantic claptrap of the Gothic novel: abduction, cruel noblemen, the sexually victimized young woman who dies in delirium, the brother's revenge attempt, the dying victim's blood curse on the evil house, the secret imprisonment of the witness. With sensational elements like this it is no wonder the story held the unruly mob in the courtroom spellbound. Yet it has two redeeming factors—the speed and vigor of the prose and the clear relation of the tale to the rest of the novel.

Chapter 10 provides a key to many unexplained mysteries. It hints at Madame Defarge's origin and motivation; it reveals the purpose of Charles Darnay's trips between France and England from 1775 to 1780; it shows his true parentage and motives; it explains the ambiguous interview Darnay held with his uncle just before the uncle was murdered; it shows how the uncle lost his influence at Court; it explains much of Manette's misery in prison after being wrenched from his pregnant wife; it explains why Manette disliked Darnay's appearance; it shows the reason for Manette's terrible shock on learning of Darnay's true identity just before the young man married his daughter. But in doing all of this the manuscript strips the plot to its very bones and makes it seem more melodramatic than it really is. The stark melodrama of this inserted tale tends to transfer its Gothic quality to the novel.

Nonetheless, the shock of these unbelievable coincidences does indicate something about Dickens' novelistic world which is very important. Coincidence is the novelist's technique for showing the workings of a Divine Providence, and it also points to the brotherhood of man. Every evil, Dickens suggests, will someday be brought to an earthly justice, and sons will have to account for their fathers' sins, just as Darnay was condemned for those of his father and uncle. His aristocratic family name, Evrémonde, nevertheless suggests Everyman and Everyworld. These coincidences show the world to be a very small place, where every action has its equal and opposite reaction. Darnay seems forced to undergo the same trial for the same crime repetitively, as in a nightmare, because he cannot escape his family history.

But this world Dickens shows us is not altogether mechanical. There is room for grace, for a change in the human heart, for a son not merely to pay for his father's sins but to redeem them. This is where Sydney Carton's sacrifice will come in. Carton, in effect, will take the sins of the Evrémondes upon himself by going to the guillotine in Darnay's place. His death will be the freely chosen sacrifice of an innocent man in the cause of love — almost in direct imitation of Christ. Darnay was sentenced to death by the Old Testament ethic of the law of talion, "an eye for an eye," even though he himself was innocent. But Carton will save him through the New Testament ethic of love and self-sacrifice, and he will pay the penalty of the law of talion. That is precisely Madame Defarge's strength; she is calling Darnay to retribution because she wants to exterminate the Evrémondes, just as they wiped out her family. This retribution has to be paid in one way or another before the New Testament ethic can take effect. That is the morality on which the action is based.

Dickens shows Sydney Carton contriving the safe escape of his friends with an exemplary thoroughness, while he is also planning to take Darnay's place. This requires great presence of mind. Behind it lies his devotion to Lucie, and yet during his three days in Paris he has not once mentioned her by name — as if naming her would profane her power for him.

Darnay's time in prison has caused Darnay's features to take on Carton's dissipated look, which increases their resemblance. (We remember that Darnay's father and uncle were twins and doubles.) The use of "doubles" was frequent in Romantic literature; Hoffman and Poe were others who employed it. For the most part, in Dickens' case the device is conventional. Darnay is of a piece throughout the novel, a man who must be rescued by his double at an ever greater price. But Dickens adds a few twists to this motif. Carton makes his double write a note to his own wife, dictating it word for word, and then places it in Darnay's pocket for Lucie. The note itself is decorous, it merely reminds Lucie of the conversation she had with Carton years ago in which he vowed to sacrifice himself for her and anyone she loved. But Carton, by making his double write the note, uses him as a conveyance, just as Darnay had used Carton to send Lucie a note at his trial in England. The favor is returned. Another irony is that by drugging Darnay, Sydney Carton reduces him to a stupefied state for the journey, a state not unlike one of Carton's alcoholic stupors. The roles have been reversed: Carton attains a new sober dignity and Darnay leaves the novel insensible.

Dr. Manette's predictable collapse has taken place, a kind of Dickensian proof that masculine pride, by itself, cannot save anyone, least of all its possessor. It is vulnerable and mortal. But Madame Defarge's power, too, is now in danger of collapse. She is more dangerous than the mob because she is utterly implacable, but vengeance has its limits as well, limits which she is unwilling to recognize in her insane determination to wipe out the whole Evrémonde family. She believes herself to be an elemental power, unstoppable as a tornado, thereby committing the sin of *hubris* — of unnatural pride. In her new self-identification with the elements she believes her power to be godlike and unconditional: "Then tell the wind and fire where to stop, but don't tell me!" Carton's repressed impulse to stab her as he leaves the shop reminds us that she is mortal. Only Carton's power, arising as it does from an unblemished love, seems invincible, even though he himself is going to die.

The acceleration of events (four days in eleven chapters) is realized only after one has come almost breathlessly to the end of the book. This increased pace expresses the intensified diabolism of the background, which gradually builds up to the revelation of sheer murderousness. This is seen in Madame Defarge's aides, who are not interested in personal revenge but in killing for its own sake, in just the number of heads that will fall from the guillotine. Dickens has chosen to illustrate precisely those elements of the Reign of Terror that anticipate the methods of totalitarian states today—the night visits of the police, the arrests on mere suspicion, the mass killings, the omnipresent fear, the public demonstrations, the mock trials. Dickens has built up his picture of total degradation very skillfully, sensing intuitively the prophetic elements of the French Revolution.

Madame Defarge dies ignominiously in a futile struggle with a woman who is just as strong and persevering as she is. This is a fight of Titans, two excessively masculine women, one representing hate and the other love. In Madame Defarge's death there is no possibility of transcendence; Sydney Carton's death, on the other hand, is victorious and serene, blessed with a vision of a better society to come and of his own survival in the son the Darnays will produce. Dickens musters all the sentiment he can in that final chapter, but it is moving nevertheless. Love, he implies, is immortal because it stems from God's eternal essence.

Dickens' Christianity is not dogmatic, and despite its sentimental trappings it is not really sentimental. However, Carton's resurrection is seen in secular terms, as a literal rebirth through Lucie and Charles Darnay. When Dickens turns to an other-worldly Heaven, as in Chapter 11, the result is unconvincing. In secularizing the promise of salvation and rendering it in worldly terms, it is as if Dickens felt that because Carton's redemption was achieved at the brink of the grave his final reward should be mundane and tangible.

Carton's redemption is prepared for, in a sense, by the redemption of Jerry Cruncher, who is truly sorry for his evildoing and who wishes unselfishly that the Darnays may safely escape. Salvation is gained on the lowest level by a sincere repentance and an unselfish hope for others. But on Carton's level, that of a total self-sacrifice for love, it is at its most sublime. It recalls Jesus' words, "Greater love hath no man than this, that a man lay down his life for his friends." This is the value that Dickens exalts and opposes to all the forces of Satanism that crowd this novel. While Dickens' literary techniques have dated somewhat in the years since this book was first published, the morality that informs those techniques could very well be relevant to our world and our situation in it.

CHARACTER ANALYSES

DR. ALEXANDRE MANETTE

Dr. Manette is imprisoned for nearly eighteen years because he has witnessed the aftermath of a crime committed by two noblemen, the Evrémondes, and has attempted to report the incident to the royal court. His incarceration and its consequences are one of the main features of the story. He can never really escape his prison experience, and in moments of great stress he reverts to the insanity which prison inflicted on him. Dr. Manette has a dual personality, an early forerunner of Stevenson's Dr. Jekyll and Mr. Hyde. Duality was a Victorian attempt to achieve complexity of character, and while the device was melodramatic, Dickens made it an integral part of the novel. Dr. Manette's character mirrors the split in society at large, a point that will be taken up later.

LUCIE DARNAY, née MANETTE

Presumably orphaned at two and brought to England by Mr. Lorry, Lucie only learns of her father's existence at seventeen, when she is summoned to rescue him with Mr. Lorry. A quiet blonde, her positive qualities are a gift for housekeeping and a compassion for unfortunates. She inspires love in almost everyone around her, but one must take this on faith because Dickens cannot bring her to life as a character. Her fainting fits and unrelenting earnestness were undoubtedly part of a Victorian concept of womanhood, in which passivity was the desired quality. Emotionally reticent for the most part, the Victorian woman (at least in fiction) tended to faint under stress. While Lucie may have been true-to-life then, the passage of time has tended to make her type obsolete both as a literary figure and as a social actuality.

CHARLES DARNAY, originally ST. EVRÉMONDE

While Darnay rejects his father and everything the Evrémondes stand for, moves to England, Anglicizes his mother's name, and renounces his inheritance, he cannot escape his family history. Trying to make amends to a missing woman whose family was wiped out by his own, he is arrested for treason in England; trying to save a jailed family servant, he is arrested in Revolutionary France, where he is tried twice. While he means well, he cannot accomplish his goals except through accident. As a character Darnay is phlegmatic and passive, and he has a penchant for getting into mortal trouble from which he has to be rescued time and again at an ever greater cost to his rescuers. With his propensity for getting jailed and tried on charges carrying the death penalty, it is no wonder Lucie falls in love with him — he is the perfect outlet for her compassion. As with her father, unjustified imprisonment seems to be his natural element.

SYDNEY CARTON

Carton, Darnay's double and alter-ego, is a frustrated alcoholic. He analyzes cases for the lawyer, Stryver, who makes a fortune picking his brains. The only noble part of his life is his chaste love for Lucie. One generally imagines Carton to be about thirty when he goes to the guillotine, but he is actually middle-aged, somewhere around forty. What gives us that illusion of youth is the adolescent nature of his love in its purity and tenacity. We tend to assume that a maturer man would have forgotten about Lucie when she married Darnay, and would have found someone else. But in Dickens' fictional world his characters may be simple, yet they have very intense attachments.

Carton takes on a mythical aspect in sacrificing himself to save his friends. He is the culture-hero who is ritually slaughtered of his own free will so that society might renew itself, a prospect he envisions before he dies. If Darnay is society's innocent victim who suffers because of the sins of his fathers, Carton is the sacrificial hero who redeems those sins in an imitation of Christ.

JARVIS LORRY

Mr. Lorry has a protective role. He takes Lucie as an infant to England, rescues her father from France, and aids the escape of his friends from Revolutionary France. A bachelor and an elderly man of business, he still has great natural affection. He is shrewd, capable, ordinarily mild-mannered, full of rectitude and fidelity — all the traits one might wish for in a fairy godfather. Yet he somehow transcends the cliché, perhaps because he, too, has to submit to his prison-like environment at Tellson's Bank.

MISS PROSS

Miss Pross is another protective figure, a big, gruff, mannish, red-haired woman with a heart of gold. She is Lucie's nurse and guardian, a role that she never fully relinquishes. Miss Pross aids the Darnays' escape from France by killing Madame Defarge in a struggle. She transcends the stereotype of the stiff, short-tempered, masculine British nanny by her somewhat excessive devotion to Lucie. A spinster, she appears to be Mr. Lorry's female complement as a character.

MADAME DEFARGE

Because her entire family perished when she was a young girl, Madame Defarge wants revenge, not merely on the family that caused the evil but on the entire class from which it came. What makes her such a threatening figure is her stubborn patience, which bides its time until it can strike. In this she is like some natural force, and when the opportunity arrives she is ferocious and unrelenting. Her secret management of Darnay's re-arrest is cunning, but it shows immense cruelty as well. In seeking to avenge her family she has acquired some of the traits of the men who did that wrong. Her knitting represents both her patience and her urge to retaliate, since she knits the names of her intended victims. As a character she serves a symbolic function in that she sums up the intensity and blood thirst behind the Revolution.

ERNEST DEFARGE

Defarge was Dr. Manette's servant as a boy, and he seems to have a filial reverence for him during the Revolution. But when the doctor was newly released from prison, Defarge was not above exploiting his insanity as a spectacle to further the revolutionary cause. As a revolutionary leader Defarge generally follows his wife, but he wants to spare the doctor, and Lucie and her daughter—a scruple that his wife interprets as weakness. We are told that in the end Defarge will go to the guillotine with all the leaders then in power.

MARQUIS ST. EVRÉMONDE

Darnay's uncle, he is a stock villain in Dickens' repertoire: the cynical, polished rake. Evrémonde is a crude class-symbol and exemplifies the predatory nature of the French aristocracy. The cause of Madame Defarge's family tragedy and of Dr. Manette's long imprisonment, his concept of honor consists of getting what you want regardless of the consequences. But he has no influence at Court and is viciously frustrated. In running over a child he provides the motive for his own murder at the hands of Gaspard, the child's father.

JERRY CRUNCHER

A porter for Tellson's by day and a body-snatcher by night, he parodies the duality of Dr. Manette in a comic way. His euphemisms create a topsy-turvy world in which body-snatching becomes respectable and prayer is degraded to "flopping." In digging up buried bodies he also turns the theme of resurrection into a ghastly parody. He serves as a lever in the plot when his knowledge of Cly's fake burial enables Sydney Carton to blackmail John Barsad effectively. And in the end Cruncher is redeemed on a minimal level. In him Dickens exhibits a wonderful craftsmanship, but the comedy is rather thin.

C. J. STRYVER

An aggressive, insensitive boor, he has succeeded in his law practice through Carton's brains and his own drive. Stryver is presented satirically, particularly in his unsuccessful courtship of Lucie Manette. Unable to take an honorable defeat, he turns it into an ignoble victory by pretending that Lucie wanted to snare him. Self-centered, he is the prototype of the coarse newly-rich.

TIME SCHEME

DATE	EVENT	BK. & CH.
Dec. 1757	Dr. Manette sees the Evrémonde crime and is imprisoned.	III, 10
Dec. 1767	Dr. Manette writes his manuscript in prison and hides it.	III, 10
Nov. 1775	Released, Manette is taken in an insane condition to England.	I, 1-6
April 1780	Darnay's trial.	II, 2-4
Aug. 1780	Sunday in Soho.	II, 6
? 1780	Darnay sees his uncle; uncle is slain.	II, 9
Aug. 1781	Darnay, Stryver, and Carton make their avowals to Lucie.	II, 10-13
	Roger Cly's funeral.	II, 14
	Defarges in France.	II, 15-16
? 1781	Darnay marries Lucie Manette; her father's relapse.	II, 17-19
? 1781	Carton visits Darnays.	II, 20
? 1783	Young Lucie born.	II, 21
July 1789	Storming of the Bastille; Revolution begins.	II, 21
July 1789	Murder of Foulon.	II, 22
? 1789	Burning of the Evrémonde château.	II, 23
Aug. 1792	Darnay goes to Revolutionary France, and is imprisoned.	II, 24 / III, 1
Sept. 1792	Dr. Manette and Lucie arrive in Paris; and Manette saves Darnay from slaughter by the mob.	III, 2 / III, 2-4
Dec. 1793	Lucie sees Carmagnole.	III, 5
	Darnay's trial; acquitted.	III, 6
	Darnay re-arrested.	III, 7
	Darnay's new trial; condemned.	III, 9-10
	Carton changes places with Darnay; Darnays escape.	III, 13
	Madame Defarge killed.	III, 14
	Carton guillotined.	III, 15

A TALE OF TWO CITIES

GENEALOGY

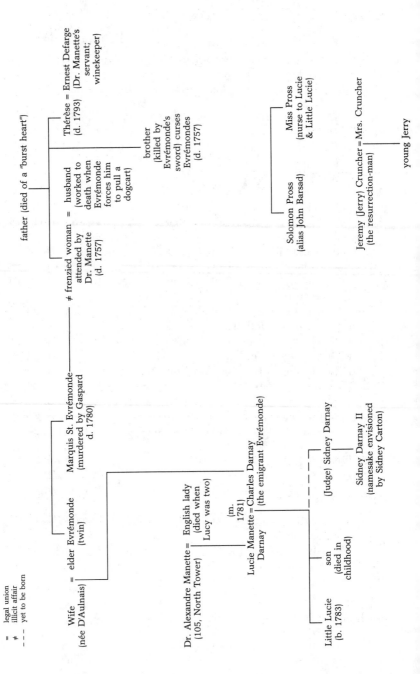

THE FRENCH REVOLUTION:
A BRIEF HISTORY

When Louis XVI became king of France, he inherited a condition of economic distress, social unrest, a debauched court, and problems with the nobility and *parlement* (the courts of justice). It was a fatal inheritance. At the time, the aristocracy were living on borrowed money and off the labors of the lower classes. The middle class were becoming wealthy from their trade, manufacturing, banking, and contracting. The lower middle class were tradesmen and laborers; a few were government officials.

The king, only twenty, was inexperienced, easily influenced, and he soon tired of his country's problems. He was a shy man and a devout Catholic. Oddly (perhaps for a king), he enjoyed repairing all sorts of locks. Otherwise, he seemed to be unhappy. He was often indecisive and tended to be narrow-minded; he usually depended on his ministers for advice, but frequently, he would reverse their decisions and decide matters for himself — simply because he wanted to show his authority. He sincerely believed that he ruled by the will of God, by the Divine Right of Kings.

The court was in debt and was in dire need of money because of years of royal extravagance, financial deficits, and two wars. In order to cope with these problems, Louis recalled the "old-style *parlements*," which were made up of aristocrats; he hoped that their sage, educated minds could solve his many problems. Unfortunately, these hand-picked aristocrats, or "notables," disapproved of the economic and tax reforms that had been suggested by Louis' Controller General of Finance, Jacques Turgot. As a result, Turgot was dismissed.

The notion of reform was not dismissed, though, by the general public because reform was in the air. The people favored the measures which Turgot had begun. Times were hard — especially for the lower classes. But the magistrates in the *parlements* believed that there was no necessity for reforms that would help the lower classes. They thought that the lower classes needed no social reforms; such people were born to bear the burdens of taxation.

In contrast, the nobility, because of their birth, were exempt from *any* taxation. Not surprisingly, therefore, the *parlements* passed numerous laws favoring the aristocracy, while the masses longed for the promised reforms based on Turgot's proposals. The king agreed with them, but unfortunately, he had instituted the *parlements*, and so he was helpless.

Very quickly, a power struggle developed between the king (who favored reform) and the nobles (who opposed reform). Ultimately, the aristocrats refused to give up *any* privileges that might be compromised because of reforms. Privilege was theirs by birth. They would compromise with their privileges *only* if they were given, in return, even more power in decision-making.

Contrary to general belief, then, the power struggle that initiated the French Revolution was not between the king and the masses; it was between the king and his nobles.

The *parlements* next asked Louis to return French rule to the Estates-General (a body that had not met since 1614), and eventually Louis gave in. The Estates-General was made up of three legal status groups, or Estates—simply called the First, Second, and Third Estate. The First Estate was made up of the clergy, usually the younger sons of the nobility. The Second Estate was made up of the nobility. And the Third Estate was made up of the working classes, plus some well-to-do merchants and professional men, lawyers, doctors, and members of the minor clergy. Under the rule of the Estates-General, only the nobility could hold public office, high ranks in the military, important posts in the government, or sit in *parlements*.

The First and Second Estates had many privileges. The Third Estate had none. The Third Estate paid taxes on income, land, property, crops, salt, tobacco, wine, cider, and even a poll tax at birth. If they sold property, they paid a sales tax on the money received and a tax on the sales tax. They provided free labor for the Crown and for the local lord, usually about three days a year. The army took their sons for six years (precisely when those sons were old enough to help with the crops), and they were forbidden to kill any animals, even if the animals came out of the forest to eat the crops.

John Locke, an English philosopher, influenced French philosophers and the men who would eventually be France's Revolutionary leaders. He believed that "the people" were sovereign and had a *natural* right to life, liberty, and the possession of property. He believed that the king ruled *only* to guarantee the rights of the people, and that the government's authority was limited to preserving these rights.

The commoners of France, overjoyed when Louis established the Estates-General were soon disappointed. Initially, they thought that they would have their "own" Estate and, thus, a voice in government policy-making, but they soon realized that they had no real power. Organizing the new Estates-General on the same principle of the 1614 concept meant one vote for each member of the Estates. Thus, the clergy and the aristocracy could easily out-vote the Third Estate, two to one—which they did, repeatedly.

Political problems continued to increase, and there were food riots because of food shortages. Rainstorms and hail ruined the crops of 1788, and people were hungry. Paris, in particular, was a crowded, densely populated city of poor people. The masses had no jobs and no money. They began burning and looting the countryside, and even common soldiers began talking against their aristocratic officers. Political pamphlets aggravated the situation by demanding that the Third Estate have a stronger voice in the government.

By the middle of June 1788, poor parish priests who belonged to the First Estate began to desert their political base and joined the Third Estate. As a result, the Third Estate finally recognized that it was the only Estate that was elected by "the people." Thus, they declared themselves to be "the National Assembly," and, first off, they banned taxes.

A famous pamphlet, *Qu'est-ce que le Tiers État?* (What Is the Third Estate?), was written by Abbé Sieyès in early 1789. Sieyès' answer, of course, was that the Third Estate was the entire *nation,* the people.

Louis was in an uncomfortable and difficult position. Recognizing the legitimacy of the National Assembly would mean surrendering his power, but *not* recognizing it might drive the Third Estate to even greater rebellion. Unfortunately, he chose to listen to Jacques Necker, his Minister of Finance, and to his queen, Marie Antoinette. He decided to oppose the National Assembly. He closed the chambers where the Assembly was to convene, but the Assembly immediately moved to an indoor tennis court. Despite the confusion, the Assembly took an oath *not* to disband until they had a constitution, and they openly defied the king. They *would* have a constitution.

Three days later, Louis vetoed the legitimacy of the National Assembly and ordered the Estates-General to return to their traditional system or he would dismiss them. When he left, the Second and most of the First Estate followed him out. The Third Estate remained, and one of them, Mirabeau, shouted that the Third Estate would leave the assembly hall "only at the point of a bayonet!" Louis could not bring himself to use force against the Estate because so many clergymen and liberal noblemen had joined them. In a dramatic move, they defied the king and won. The Revolution had begun.

Paris, always a hotbed of dissension, had a large populace that was ready to fight against almost anything. In every corner, people seemed to be meeting and conspiring; everywhere, people talked of revolution. Hunger haunted the city, and bread shortages were a constant threat. Grain shipped into the city was often stolen before it arrived, and in the early summer of 1789, bread riots broke out.

Because the thousands of workers' salaries could not possibly keep pace with soaring prices, workers began wrecking factories and burning property. At this point, the Swiss Guard marched into Paris in early July and immediately rumors spread that the aristocrats were going to try to stop the Revolution by armed force. In fact, however, Louis simply stationed the Swiss Guard where he did because the French Guard refused to fight against their own countrymen.

Four days before the Bastille fell, Louis dismissed Necker and the rest of his cabinet and appointed a new council of anti-revolutionary royalists. Almost immediately, there were rumors that the Swiss Guard and the German Guard were ready to murder the Parisian populace. Even the French Guard believed the rumors. They joined the rioting masses and broke into the Tuileries Palace, taking gunpowder and ornamental guns and a cannon. Rioting and looting continued, and small shops and government buildings were broken into and destroyed.

On July 14, a mob of citizens seized 30,000 muskets from the Invalides and attacked the Bastille, where the royal store of gunpowder was kept. They hung and butchered the governor and his guards and released the few prisoners who were there. Strangely enough, the mob still had a sympathetic feeling for

Louis; they had lost all respect for him as a king, but they still felt affection for him.

In fact, the masses weren't as afraid of Louis as they were afraid of the cluster of noblemen who surrounded him. They were paranoid about royalist schemes to quash the Revolution, and so they looted and burned chateaus throughout the country-side. Landlords were slaughtered simply because they were landlords. Consequently, aristocrats began leaving France in droves; the country was no longer safe unless you were a ragged revolutionary. These uprisings and the general climate were part and parcel of the "Great Fear."

On August 4, the National Assembly passed a measure denying all feudal rights of the aristocracy. But even that measure did little to help the constant, painful problem of hunger. The masses were no better off. The National Assembly could do nothing to provide food or lower prices. And, of course, the aristocracy was blamed for the bread shortages, largely because the counter-revolutionaries were holding lavish banquets at Versailles.

Finally, a band of women decided to march on Versailles. Louis' advisor Lafayette was in a quandry as how to handle the situation, so he decided to send troops to "protect" the women. Meanwhile, the women continued their march, looting shops along the way and sharpening their knives on the stones (mile stones), talking of the numerous ways that they might torture Queen Marie Antoinette.

Walking through the rain, dripping wet, the women arrived at the Assembly. The legislators attempted to do business with the women, but they were wringing out their clothes and creating such a hubbub that nothing was accomplished. Shouting obscenities, they said that they would listen to only Mirabeau and Robespierre. Finally the Assembly sent a delegation of the women to Louis, warning them to watch their language. Louis graciously received them and promised to give them grain. Then some of them attempted to murder the queen. Next morning, Louis and his family were escorted to the Tuileries, a former palace of the kings of France.

Louis, in effect, moved the government from Versailles to Paris, and, as a result, almost half of his nobles chose to go into exile rather than face the chaotic revolutionaries of Paris.

The mob was divided; some of them wanted a constitutional monarchy with an Assembly making the laws; others wanted to return to a monarchy. Still others, of course, wanted to depose Louis. These groups were wild and unorganized. Confusion and pandemonium reigned.

The Assembly decided to divide France into 83 departments, giving considerable freedom to all of the departments. Then they passed a new law which, ironically, caused an even greater schism between the classes. The new law stated that *anyone* could vote—*if* they had paid their taxes. The peasants felt betrayed; they had no money to pay taxes. They were already taxed to death. The Revolution was doing absolutely nothing for them.

After Louis had been in Paris for awhile, he and his family planned to flee to Metz, near the Rhine frontier, but problems along the way delayed the royal escape. The guard who was to help them on the final lap of their route failed to show up. He had heard a rumor that the king had already been captured, and he feared for his life. Thus the king was captured. He was recognized at the small post station of Varennes, and he and the royal family were returned to Paris under arrest. Unfortunately, the king left behind him innumerable documents stating his views about the Revolution and the proposed new constitution.

Louis was suspended from power until he signed the new constitution and accepted his role as only a "constitutional monarch." Robespierre denounced him, and the *sans-culottes,* a group of small businessmen, laborers, artisans, as well as the very poor, demanded his removal. In addition, they called for a Republic.

A period of virtual terror began. Its leaders were Robespierre and the *sans-culottes*. The latter were rough, hard-headed men, and they threatened violence in order to gain power. A rally at the Champ de Mars ended in a bloody massacre for them, and Robespierre went into hiding;, but their cause persisted, for when the new Assembly met, there were *no* monarchists present.

The new government began issuing paper money as legal tender because it associated gold with aristocrats and the wealthy. Exiled nobles, therefore, flooded France with forged paper money, adding to the already deflated money value. Food prices continued to rise, and even two years of good harvests failed to alleviate the hunger of the masses. Hoarders held their grain from the market, and merchants exported their grain, hoping to make more money. Mobs began raiding and robbing supply convoys. Soap was in short supply, and sugar was disappearing. Food riots began again.

At this point, the Girondists, who made up the right wing of the newly organized government, came into power, but instead of attacking financial problems and food shortages, they tackled the problem of counter-revolutionaries. During this counter-revolutionary period, many of the lessons of the French Revolution are seen. A feeling of great inspiration overwhelmed the men, women, and children of France. They felt as though their state was in danger of total collapse. The theme of "liberty, equality, and fraternity" could be heard, and the *Marseillaise* became the French National anthem. It is at this point of the French Revolution that students of history begin to draw significant meaning. This feeling for the "general will" of the French government created a new revolutionary ideology. Most people seemed to be positively inspired by the rightful meaning of their cause. The French Revolution produced a multi-faceted term called Modern Nationalism, and while modern nationalism can be interpreted in so many different ways, its primary ideology can be felt through the nineteenth- and twentieth-century development of Europe.

To detract from the domestic problem, the Girondists declared war on Austria and Belgium. Louis thought that the declaration of war would cause the counter-revolutionaries to join with Austria and that his throne would eventually be saved. He knew that France was not ready for war and that many of the aristocratic officers had deserted. He was right. After the first encounter with the enemy, the French armies' lack of ammunition and supplies became all too obvious. Thus the French generals ordered retreat. The soldiers, crying treason, took revenge on those generals.

Afterward, the Girondists blamed Louis for the defeat, and they called the Swiss Guard to Paris for their protection. The Girondists were fast losing power and popularity, and eventually the *sans-culottes* sent an ultimatum to the Assembly to depose the king by August 9 or they would overthrow the government by force.

During the battle between the *sans-culottes* and the Swiss Guard, Louis and his family fled to the National Assembly for protection. The Assembly asked Louis to order the Swiss Guard to cease fire. The Guard ceased firing, and the mob slaughtered them. Then it proceeded to smash windows and destroy furniture. An orgy of destruction had begun. The Assembly deposed Louis, put him and his family under arrest, and sent him to prison in the Knights Templars temple on August 13, 1792.

Danton, a popular rebel, now became the new Minister of Justice. He urged the French people to join the army and save France. With most of the able-bodied men gone from Paris, Marat, eager for power, spread the rumor that the imprisoned aristocrats and priests were ready to break out and take their revenge on the masses. It was a ridiculous idea. Four hundred men could never overcome a city of half a million. But the people feared everything, even the impossible.

The priests were moved to another prison, and in the process, an unruly mob turned into a frenzy and butchered them. The mob then moved on to other prisons, murdering more than 300 prisoners. The blood bath continued and, on the following day, they killed 1,100 people—and less than thirty were aristocrats. Most of those murdered were criminals, women, beggars, and children.

The Girondists held power only a little longer. They lost it to the Jacobins and the *sans-culottes*, who called for the death of the king. Louis was guillotined on January 21, 1793.

Louis' death solved nothing. There was still no food, and riots and plundering by the *sans-culottes* further weakened the already-weak governing structure. Eventually, the Jacobins and the *sans-culottes* took complete control. Setting up a Revolutionary Tribunal, they made despotic decisions—from which no appeal was possible.

Robespierre then took control of the Revolution, and the "Reign of Terror" began. He was a champion of "the people's rights," but he could not understand why food and better wages were more important to the masses than dedication to the principles of a free France. He saw traitors and plotters everywhere, and anyone disagreeing with him became a traitor. He convinced his colleagues to believe that force and terror were essential to the preservation of a safe society.

Robespierre, however, was beset by problems. The British had blockaded the French ports; the country was in a state of famine, and trade and industry were at a standstill. In the south of France, the counter-revolutionaries were threatening, and to the north, war with Belgium threatened.

Hundreds were executed at Marseilles and Toulon; nearly two thousand were drowned in the Loire River at Nantes; over fifteen hundred were condemned to death, and if the guillotine worked too slowly, they slaughtered the victims with firing squads or else they blew them to bits with cannons.

In August, the queen was taken to prison. She was tried in October and was guillotined on October 16, 1793.

The Revolutionary Tribunal was divided into four courts, which sat day and night. By September, the "Law of Suspects" had created so many "accused" people that the court tried cases in groups of fifty. Courts tried everyone: priests, hoarders, swindlers, aristocrats, and, of course, innocent men and women. Neighbor turned in neighbor. In all, over twenty-five thousand people were killed during the "Reign of Terror."

Fear was rampant—in *all* classes. Even the lower and middle classes feared that a simple, casual comment might send them to the guillotine. In fact, more people from the lower and middle classes were being guillotined than the entire group of aristocrats, generals, and public officials. The Revolution was "eating its own children."

In the provinces, there was a nightmare of fear. Priests were imprisoned, churches were looted and destroyed, and there was such a bloodbath that some of the Jacobins returned to Paris in disgust.

The *sans-culottes* closed all the churches in Paris; they even took over Notre Dame Cathedral for an atheistic "Feast of Reason." Robespierre was unhappy with this decision but his followers were equally unhappy with his "police bureau," which was more eager than ever to bring in accused people for a quick trial and an even quicker trip to the guillotine. Eventually, they began plotting Robespierre's downfall, and eventually they accused him—just as he had accused others. He was sent to the guillotine after an unsuccessful suicide attempt.

After Robespierre's death, France moved into a period called the Thermidorian reaction, a relatively quiet period. The new government was called the Directory. It was an inefficient and corrupt government, but nevertheless it did provide a relatively stable regime. Nobility who had fled France began to return—namely, Talleyrand, who was appointed foreign minister. Unfortunately, the new government put Napoleon Bonaparte in charge of its army. Unwittingly, it was replacing the country's terrorists with someone who soon be a virtual dictator.

NOTES

NOTES

NOTES

NOTES